CIRQUE DU S

A NEW MUSICAL COLLECTION

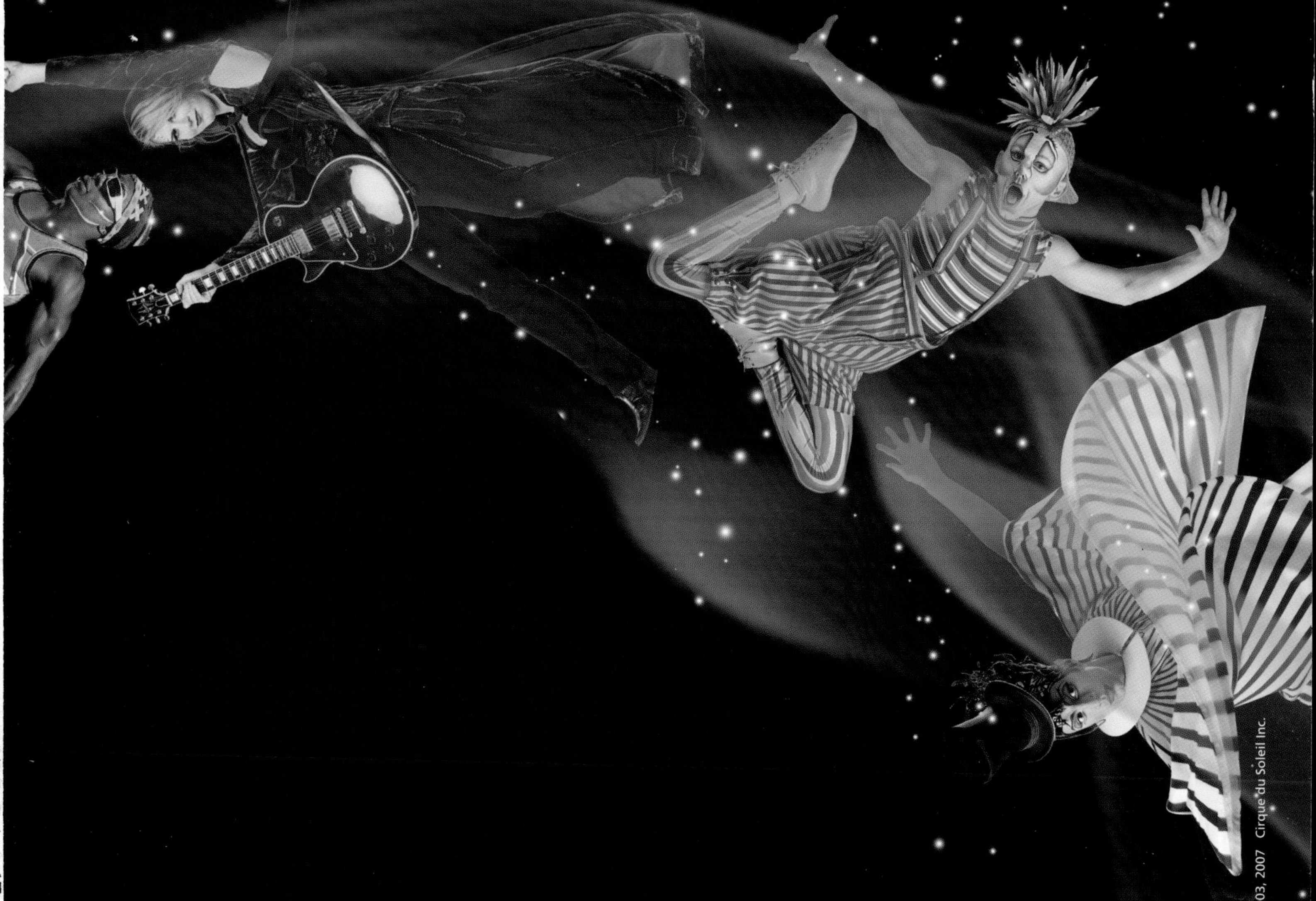

Produced by
Alfred Music
P.O. Box 10003
Van Nuys, CA 91410-0003
alfred.com

Printed in USA.

ISBN-10: 1-4706-1705-6
ISBN-13: 978-1-4706-1705-9

BLUE SILK
(from *ZED*)

Music by
RENÉ DUPÉRÉ

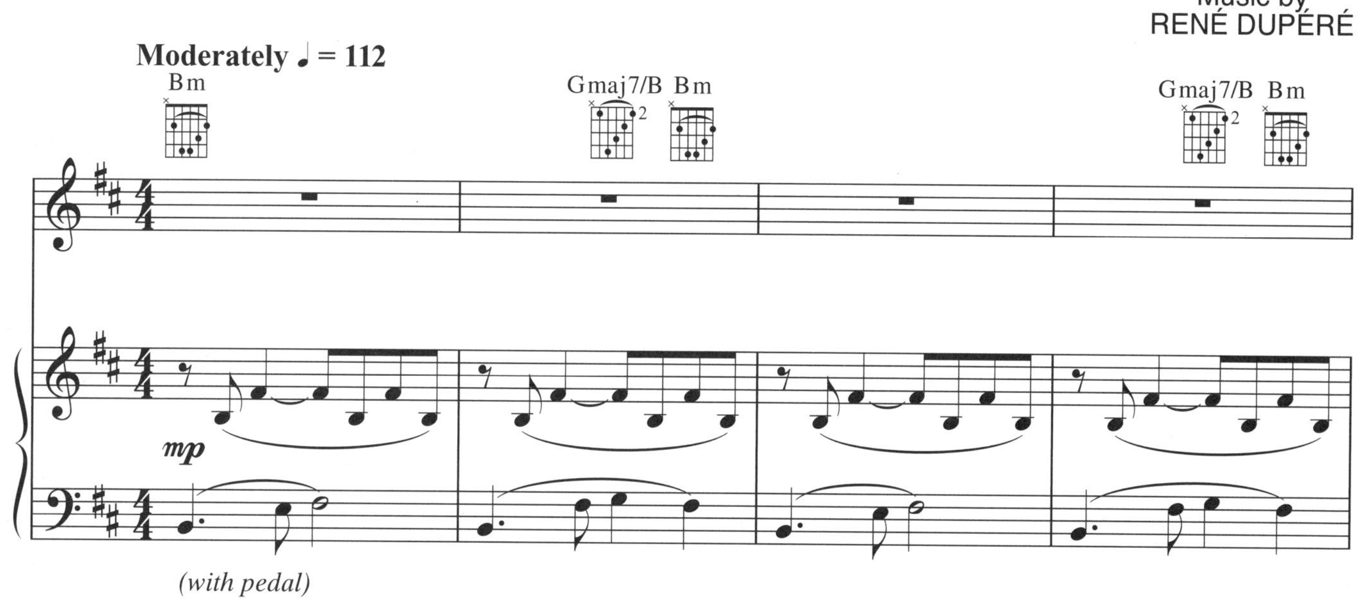

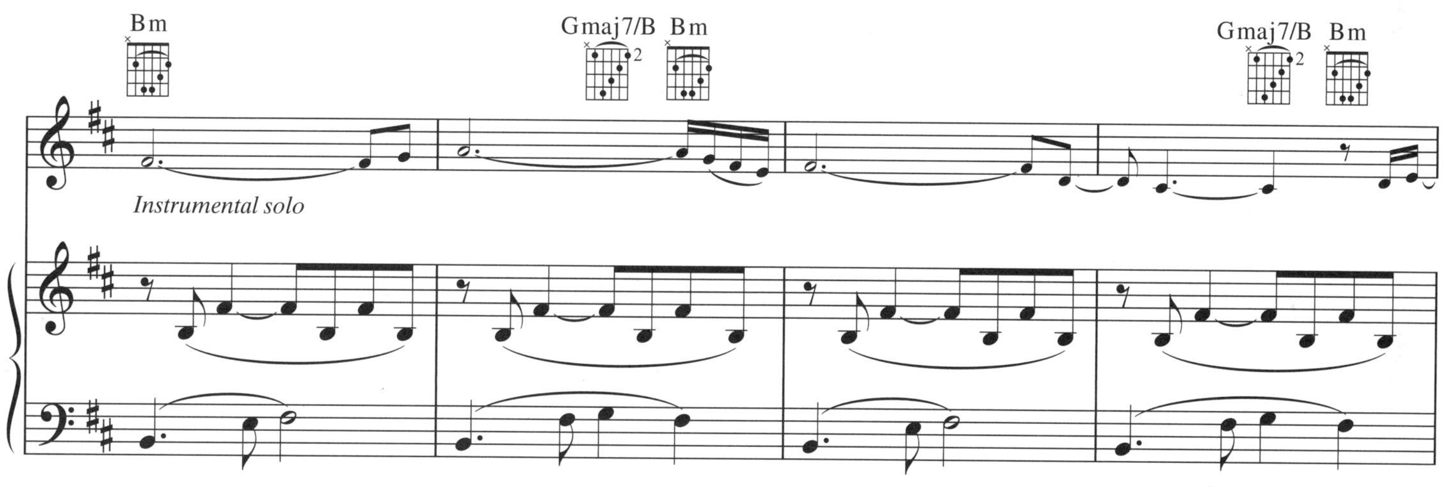

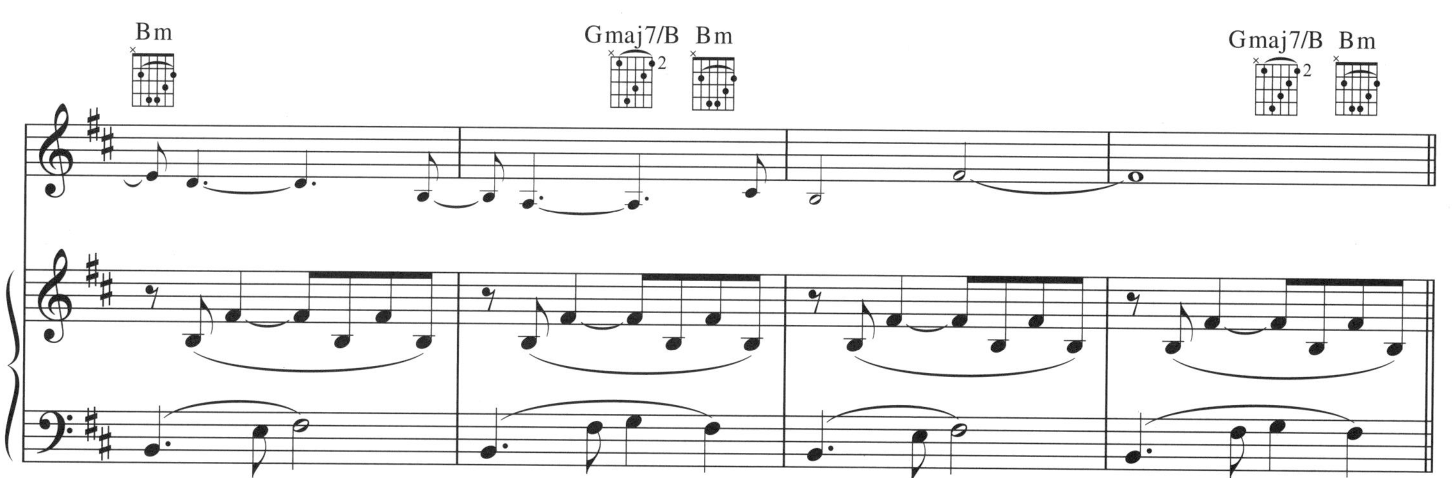

Verse 1:
Bm
Bm(maj7)
Bm7
Man:
1. Ka tchi na va me - la ke tchay le
Gmaj7/B
Bm
va shin ha.
G
A
D
Woman:
Tchoy ka tchi na mo ve ta ke sho ve.
F♯m
Bm
Bm(maj7)
Man:
Ka me ko tche no va ke

Bm7
Gmaj7/B
Bm
ma run de ke va.
G
A
Woman:
Laï no va lei a she ko,
D
D/F♯
Chorus:
G
A
G/B
Man + Woman:
sha ve.
La ki va ve la,
G
A
G/B
A
Bm
A/C♯
A
Bm
A/C♯
la ki va ve la,
la ki va ve la,
la ki va ve la,

Bm
G
A
G/B
ke va.
La ki va ve la,
A/C♯
la ki va ve la,
la ki va ve la,
la ki va ve la,
ke va,
ke la.
Instrumental solo

G
A
G
A
Bm7
A/C♯
F♯m7
Verse 2:
Bm
Bm(maj7)
Bm7
Man:
2. Ka tchi na va me - la ke tchay le
Gmaj7/B
Bm
va shin ha.

G A D
Woman:
Tchoy ka tchi na mo ve ta ke sho ve.
Chorus:
D/F♯ G A G/B G A G/B
Man +
Woman:
La ki va ve la, la ki va ve la,
A Bm A/C♯ A Bm A/C♯ Bm
la ki va ve la, la ki va ve la, ke va.
G A G/B G A G/B
La ki va ve la, la ki va ve la,

A Bm A/C♯ A Bm A/C♯ Bm

la ki va ve___ la, la ki va ve___ la, ke va,___

___ ke la.___

Gmaj7/B Bm Gmaj7/B Bm

Instrumental solo

G A Bm

A/C♯
D
Em7
Bm
Gmaj7/B
Bm
Gmaj7/B
Bm
Freely
cadenza
Bm
Bm/A
Gmaj7
D/F♯
Em

Gmaj7/D
C♯m7(♭5)
G/B
A♯dim
rall.
Bm
Gmaj7/B
Bm
a tempo
Gmaj7/B
Bm
Bm
Gmaj7/B
Bm
Gmaj7/B
Bm

ALEGRÍA
(from *Alegría*)

Lyrics by
FRANCO DRAGONE, MANUEL TADROS
and CLAUDE AMESSE

Music by
RENÉ DUPÉRÉ

Verse:
Dm
1.(3.) A - le - grí - a, co - me un
(2.) grí - a, I see a
4. See additional lyrics
mf
F
C
Dm
lam - po di vi - ta, a - le - grí - a. Co - me un
spark of life shin - ing, a - le - grí - a. I hear a
F
C
Dm
pa - zzo gri - dar, a - le - grí - a. Del de - lit -
young min - strel sing, a - le - grí - a. Beau - ti - ful
F
C
Dm
B♭
Am
tuo - so gri - do, bel - la rug - gen - te pe - na, se -
roar - ing stream, of joy and sor - row, so ex -

Gm7
F
C
ren.
Co-me la ra - bia__ di a - mar, a-le -
treme.
There is a love in__ me rag - ing, a-le -
Dm
B♭
F
C
grí - a,__ co-me un as - sal - to__ di gio -
grí - a,__ a joy-ous, mag - i - cal feel -
1.2.
Dm
F
C
Dm
B♭
ia.
ing.
(Instrumental solo)
F
C
Dm
2.3. A-le -

3.4.
Dm F C
ia. Del de - lit - tuo - so gri - do, bel - la rug -
dad. Del e - stu - pen - do gri - to de la tris -
Dm B♭ Am Gm7
gen - te pe - na, se - ren. Co - me la
te - za lo - ca se - re - na. Co - mo la
F C Dm B♭
ra - bia di a - mar, a - le - grí - a. Co - me un as -
ra - bia de a - mar, a - le - grí - a. Co - mo un a -
F C
1.
Dm
D.S.
sal - to di gio - ia. 4. A - le -
sal - to de fe - li - ci -

2.
Dm
F
C
dad.
There is a love in me rag - ing, a - le -
Dm
B♭
F
C
Dm
grí - a, a joy-ous, mag - i - cal feel - ing.
decresc.
mp
F
C
(Instrumental solo)

Verse 4:
Alegría, como la luz de la vida, alegría.
Como un payaso que grita, alegría.
Del estupendo grito,
De la tristeza loca serena.
Como la rabia de amar, alegría
Como un asalto de felicidad.

ALL COME TOGETHER

(from *Amaluna*)

Lyrics by
BOB & BILL
(GUY DUBUC and MARC LESSARD)
FERNAND RAINVILLE and ALAIN VINET

Music by
BOB & BILL
(GUY DUBUC and MARC LESSARD)

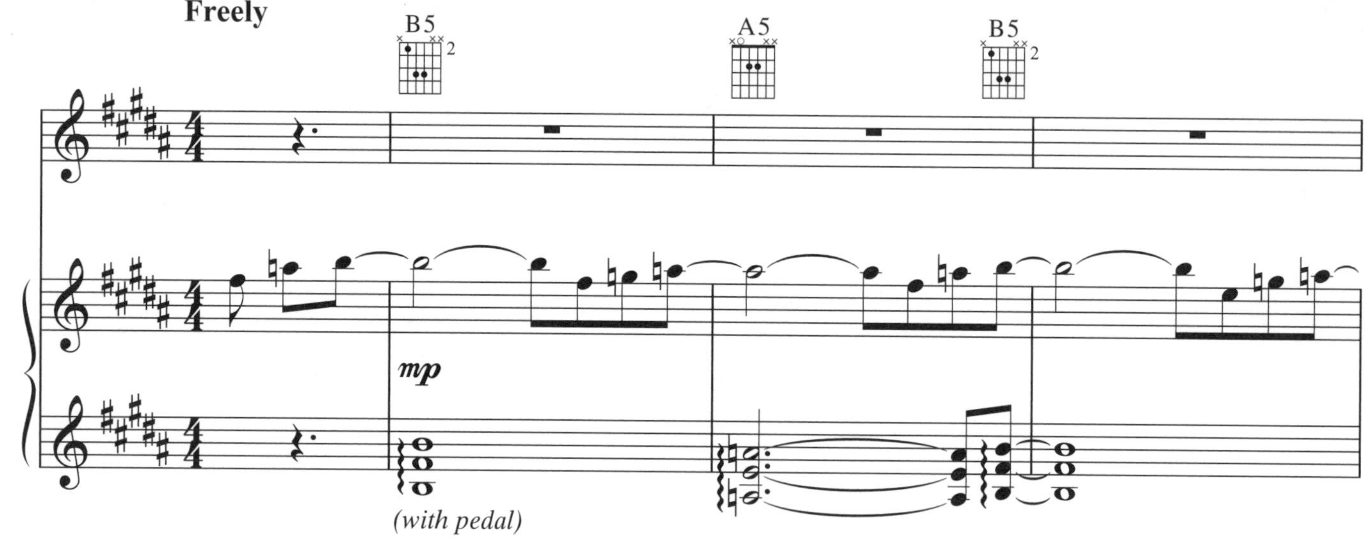

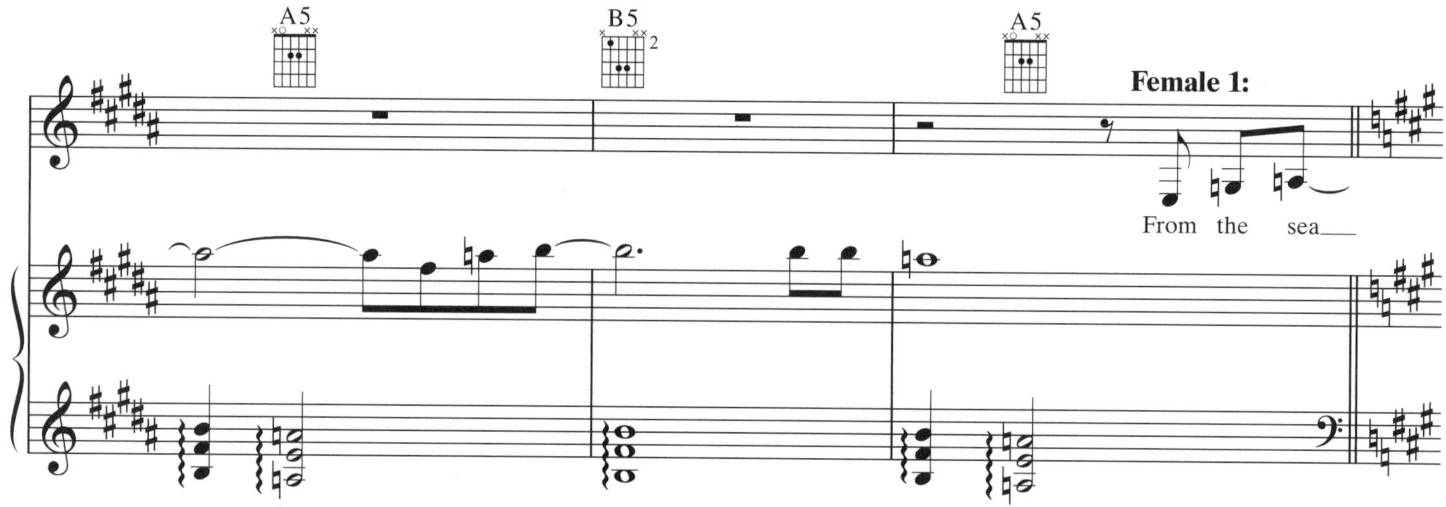

F6
Asus
A
F6
free, you and I as we all come to -
D
F
Asus
A
geth - er. From the wind, through the
F6
Asus
A
F6
rain, can you feel that we are free with the world
Asus
A
F6
D
as we all come to - geth - er.

A little faster ♩ = 110
F
A
F6
A
F6
A
F6
D
mf
Female 2:
A
F6
From the sea to the moon, through the light
A
F6
A
we shall be free, you and I as we all

F6
D
come to - geth - er, ooh. From a dream
A
F
A
through a world look up - on the o - ver -
F
A
F
flow we call love as we all come to - geth-
D
D5
5
F
er.

D5
Gsus
G
D5
F
D5
F
A
F6
From the sea to the moon, through the light
A
F6
A
we shall be free, you and I as we all
F6
D
F
come to - geth - er. From the wind,

A F6 A

through the rain, can you feel that we are

F6 A F6

free with the world as we all come to - geth-

D F A

er.

F6 A F6 A

F6
D
F
Female 2:
From the sea
A
F6/C
A
to the moon, through the light we shall be
Female 3:
From the sea, to the moon, through the light
F6/C
A
F6
free, you and I as we all come to - geth-
we shall be free, you and I, to - geth-

D F A

er. From the sea, to the moon,

Female 1:

er. From the sea,

F6/C A F6/C

through the light, we shall be free, you and I,

to the moon, through the light, we shall be free,

A F6/C D

as we all come to - geth - er.

you and I, to - geth - er.

F
Bright rock ♩ = 130
A
F/A
A
F/A
A
F/A
D
F
Female 2:
From the sea
A
F/A
A
to the moon,
through the light
we shall be

F/A
A
F/A
free, you and I as we all come to - geth-
D
F
A
er. From the sea, to the moon,
F/A
A
F/A
through the light, we shall be free, you and I,
A
F/A
D
as we all come to - geth - er.

F
A
F/A
A
F/A
A
F/A
D
F
Female 2:
From the sea,
A
F/A
A
to the moon,
through the light,
we
shall
be
Female 2:
From the sea,
to the moon,
through the light

F/A
A
F/A
free,
you and I,
as we all
come
to - geth-
we shall be free,
you and I,
to - geth-
D
F
Moderate rock ♩ = 92
er.
er.
Asus
A
F
Asus
A
F
mf
Asus
A
F
D
F

ALONE

(from *DELIRIUM*)

Lyrics by
ROBBIE DILLON and
MANUEL TADROS

Music by
RENÉ DUPÉRÉ

A7
Dm
F♯dim7
free from ha - tred and love.
in a world of my own,
Watch - ing life slow-ly
as a heart slow-ly
Gm
B♭/F
Em7(♭5)
A7
Dm
A7sus
pass me by.
turns to stone.
A - lone,
A - lone,
soar - ing o - ver the
no hel - lo, no good-
Dm
A7sus
Dm
ground,
bye,
with my head in the clouds,
watch - ing dreams as they die.
D7
Gm
F/A
here where no one can see me.
They're still there when you close your eyes.
1.2. I

Chorus:
B♭
C/B♭
Am7
fly,
look - ing down from the sky,
3. (Instrumental solo…
Dm
Dm7
Gm
Gm7
C7
on a world that's so small.
You can't touch me__ at
Fmaj7
B♭maj7
E7sus
A7
Dm
all,________ I'm too high.
A - lone,
A7sus
Dm
A7
peo - ple laugh - ing be - low,
watch - ing life from a - bove,
laugh - ter I'll nev - er
free from ha - tred and

Dm
F♯dim7
Gm
B♭/F
know, tears my eyes have re - fused to cry,
love, watch - ing life slow-ly pass me by,
Em7(♭5)
A7
To Coda
Dm
A7sus
be - fore too long.
for - ev - er - more.
…end solo)
1.
2.
D.S. al Coda
Dm
A7sus
Dm
Dm/C
Oh.
Coda
Dm
B♭
Gm6
Dm/A
A7sus
Dm
B♭
Gm6
Dm/A
A7sus
A7
Dm

BANQUETE
(from *OVO*)

Music and Lyrics by
BERNA CEPPAS

Em
F♯
bem, ca - dê, ca - dê vo - cê? Eu vim eu vim eu vim eu vim so - men - te pra te
Bm
Em
ver. Meu bem ca - dê? Coi - sin - ha
F♯7(♭9)
8
Bm
lin - da ca - dê. Meu bem, ca - dê, ca - dê vo -
Em
F♯
Bm
cê? Eu vim eu vim eu vim eu vim a - qui só pra te ver. Che -

F♯
Bm
F♯
guei não tin - ha pron - de ir. Te ol - hei não pu - de re - sis -
Bm
F♯
Bm
tir. Son - hei o quan - to con - se - gui, a - gor - a cê é
Em
F♯
Bm
B/D♯
Em7
meu é não vai me es - ca - pu - lir. O - K. A - gor - a tá na
A
F♯m
Bm
ho - ra de se di - ver - tir, je t'aime mon a - mour, te a - mo ma chér - ie,

Em6
A
D
va - mos to - dos fes - te - jar.
D♯dim7
Em7
A
O a - mor, que é a coi - sa mais bon - i - ta que po - de ex - is - tir,
F♯m
Bm
Em6
je t'aime mon a - mour I love you, ma chér - ie, va - mos co -
A
F♯
mer, be - ber, dan - çar. Chér -

Bm
Em
F♯
ie, ca - dê, ca - dê vo - cê? Je suis ve - nu i - ci, i - ci, i - ci te re - trou -
ver. Chér - ie, ca - dê, ca - dê vo - cê? Je suis ve - nu i -
ci, i - ci, i - ci pour t'em - bras - ser. Chu chu, où es -
Em6
F♯7(♯9)
tu? Co - is - a lin - da ca - dê? Chér -

Em F♯

ie, ca - dê, ca - dê vo - cê? Je suis ve - nu i - ci, i - ci, i - ci pour un bai -

Bm Em7 A7

ser. O mun - do_é min - ha_mai - son, your eyes two shin - ing

F♯m7 Bm Em

stars. Cher - che mi co - ra - zõn, que_eu ten - ho

G6 F♯ Bm

tan - to pra te dar. Vo - cê é_co - mo a

Em7
A7
F♯m7
á - gua,
não po - de me fal - tar.
Bm
Em
G6
O meu a - mor não pa - ra co - mo o ri - o dà no
F♯
Instrumental solo:
Bm
mar.
F♯7
Bm
F♯7

Bm F♯7 Bm
F♯7 Bm F♯7
8va
(8va)
Bm F♯7 Bm
F♯7 Bm F♯7
(8va)
loco
Bm B/D♯ Em7 A
4
O - K. Tu sa - is main - te - nant le temps de s'a - mus - er,

F♯m
Bm
Em6
tem - po de man - ger, tem - po de dan - ser,
c'est le
A
D
D♯dim7
temps de cé - lé - brer.
Le mon-de est ma mai -
Em7
A
F♯m
son,
your eyes two shin - ing stars,
Bm
Em
G6
cher - che mi co - ra - zõn,
qui é - tait là au - près de

F♯
Em7
toi.
Vous ê - tes com - me l'eau,
A
F♯m
Bm
qui tom - be sur la terre.
Com - me les eaux d'un
Em
A
F♯
fleu - ve qui se jet - tent dans la mer,
F♯m
dans la mer,
dans la mer.
molto rit.

FLYING SCARLETT

(from *IRIS - A Journey Through the World of Cinema*)

Music by
DANNY ELFMAN

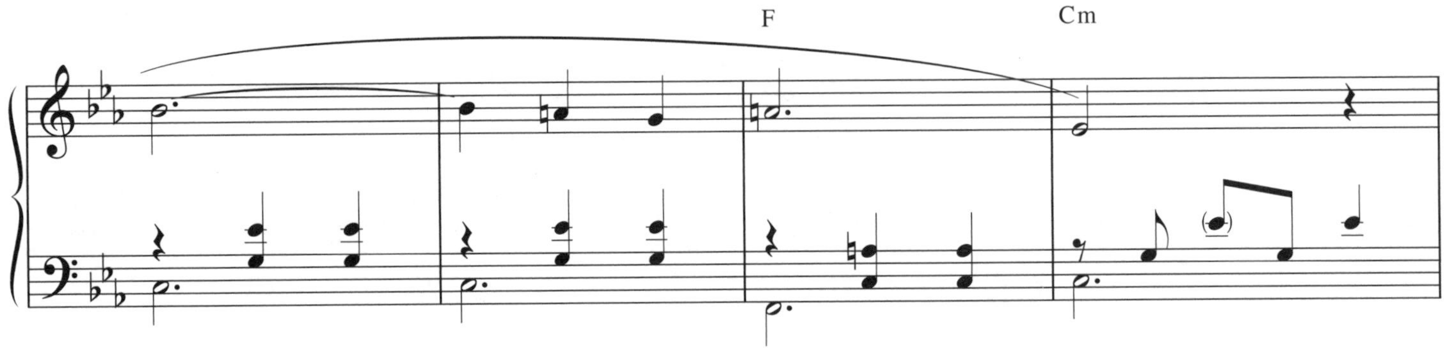

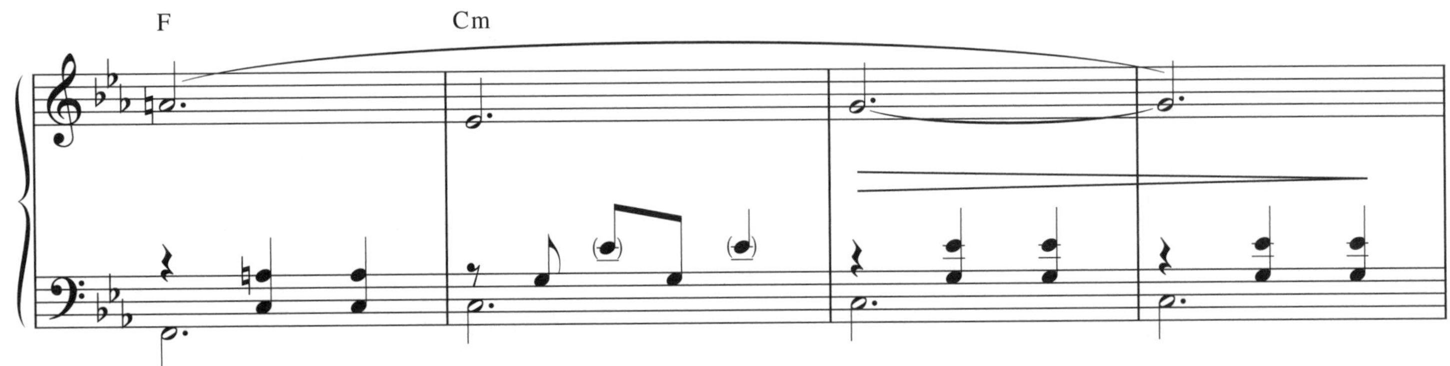

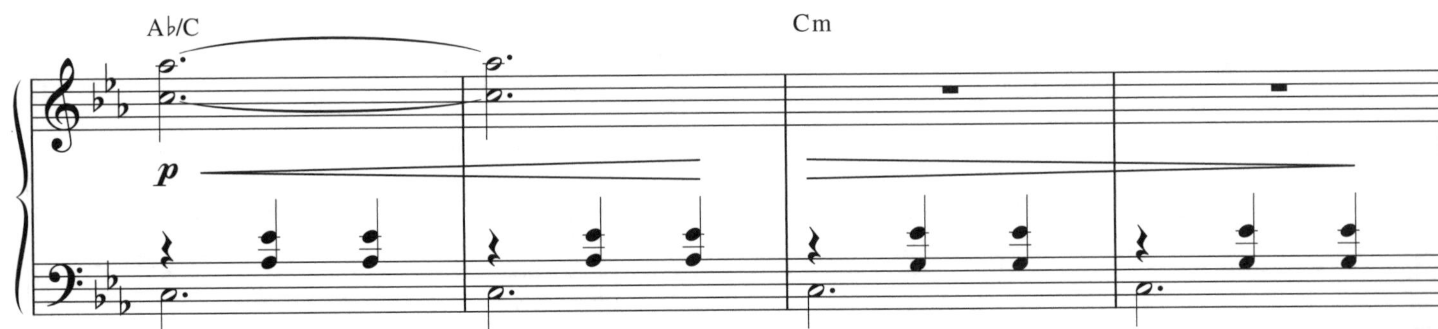

p
mp
F
Cm
F
Cm
A♭
Fm
mf
Cm/E♭
B♭
Gm
A♭
E♭
p

Fm
A♭
Cm
B♭
p
mp
F/A
F
Cm
p
3
mp
F
Cm
F
Cm
Cm(9)
Cm
Cm(9)
8va
p

(8va) F7 Cm

F7 Cm A♭ (8va) 8va mp

(8va) Fm Cm/E♭

B♭/D (8va) Cm B♭6

Cm Cm(4)

Cm
Cm7/B♭
F7/A
N.C.
Dm
Am/D
Dm
mp
Am/D
Dm
Am7/D
Dm
Am7/D
G/D
Dm7
mf
G
Dm
G

Dm
B♭
f
Dm
mf
G
Dm
G
Dm
B♭
Gm
f

Dm/F
C/E
C
Am
Dm
mp
Am7
mf
D
Am
D
Am
F

Am
Am7
D
Am
D
Am
F
Dm
Am/C
G/B
/A
G6
G6/B
Am
mp

Em
p
Em7
A
Em
mf
A
Em
Em/G
Em
C/E
f
Em

Em7
mp
A
Em
A
Em
C
Em/B
D/A
B7
B
rit.
Em(9)
a tempo
rit.
p

GAMELAN
(from «O»)

Music by
BENOIT JUTRAS

Ma - sai - yah yon - ta - la. Ma - sai - yah yon - ta - la
beh.
So - be -
E♭m
6
N.C.
(modal outline, Dorian in nature.)
yah ton-yah ko - ton - ya leh. So - be - yah so - beh a - leh. Ko - ba -
3

da na na tu - ma - la a - 'a - na nin - de. So-be -
yah ton-yah ko - ton - ya leh. So - be - yah so - be a - leh. Tu - ma -
la ton-yah a - na ni - be ko - be - na tium - ba - le, ton -
yah.
p (as bells)

Fm7(♭5) Bbsus

mp

Fm7(♭5) Bbsus Bb

So-be -

cresc.

Ebm N.C. (Dorian mode)

yah kon-ya ko - ton-ya leh.___ So-be - ya so-be___ a - leh.___ Ko-ba -

mf

da na___ na tu - ma - la___ a - 'a - na nin - de.___

Ma - sai - yah yon - ta - la. Ma - sai-yah yon - ta - la.
Ma - sai - yah yon - ta - la. Ma - sai - yah
Fm7(♭5)
yon - ta - la beh.
dim.
mp
Ma - sai - yah yon - ta - la. Ma - sai-yah yon - ta - la.
B♭sus

G♭
D♭
E♭m
C♭
So - be kunadun - se, ko - re go ni - ma - ya ku - ro to.
f
So - be ko - na dun - se, ko - re go ni - ma - sun - ge. Dao ko-meh.
So - be ku - na dun - se, ko - re swe - go - noi - ya ni - mo to.
B♭sus
To Coda
So - be ku - na dun - se, ko - re go ni - ma - ya leh

B♭
E♭m
6
chla.
mp
Interlude:
Cm
3
Gm
3
A♭
4
B♭
mf
Cm
3
Gm
3
A♭
4
B♭
Cm
3
Gm
3
A♭
4
B♭

Cm
Gm
A♭
B♭
A♭maj7
mp
E♭m
D.S. 𝄋 al Coda
mf
𝄌 Coda
B♭
G♭
D♭
E♭m
chla. So - be ku - na dun - se, ko - re go ni - ma - ya ku -
(Vocal ad lib. underneath)
f

C♭
G♭
D♭
E♭m
ro to. So - be ko - na dun - se, ko - re go ni - ma - sun - ge.
sim.
C♭
G♭
D♭
E♭m
Dao ko - meh. So - be ku - na dun - se, ko - re swe - go - noi - ya ni -
C♭
G♭
D♭
E♭m
mo to. So - be ku - na dun - se, ko - re go ni - ma - ya leh
B♭sus
B♭
B♭sus
B♭
N.C.
chla.

KUMBALAWÉ
(from *Saltimbanco*)

Music by
RENÉ DUPÉRÉ

E♭
A♭
Verse:
E♭
A♭maj7
1.3.4. Kum - ba - la - wé ma - na, kum - ba - la - wé ma - na, u - ru - li - mé.
2. (Instrumental)
mf
E♭
Kum - ba - la - wé ma - na, kum - ba - la - wé ma - na,
A♭maj9
E♭
u - ru - li - mé. Te - ku man - de m'ba - la,

A♭
te - ku man - de m'ba - la, te - ku man - de. Kum - ba - la - wé
E♭
A♭
ma - na. Kum - ba te - ku man - de.
Bridge:
Cm
A♭
E♭/G
Ke - run - da, ke - run - da n' - zan - ye. Ke - run - da, ke - run - da m'ba - gi - re.
B♭
A♭
Kum - ba - la we - ge, kum - ba - la we - ge, a - za - ma - ny - ki

E♭
Cm
A♭
run da-we.
Ke - run-da, ke - run - da n'-zan-ye. Ke -
E♭/G
B♭
A♭
run - da, ke - run - da m'ba - gi - re.
Kum - ba - la we - ge, kum - ba - la
E♭
1.2.3.
we - ge, a - za - ma - ny - ki run da - we.
4.
A♭
Kum - ba - la we - ge, kum - ba - la we - ge, a - za - ma - ny - ki

E♭
A♭
4
run da - we.
Kum - ba - la we - ge, kum - ba - la
E♭
we - ge, a - za - ma - ny - ki run da - we.
N.C.
Kum - ba - la - wé ma - na, kum - ba - la - wé ma - na,
1.2.3.
4.
u - ru - li - mé.
u - ru - li - mé.

IF I COULD REACH YOUR HEART

(from *KÀ*)

Lyrics by
ELLA

Music by
RENÉ DUPÉRÉ

D

If___ I___ could reach your heart__ with those
If___ I___ could see your soul__ when you

Bm7 G A7sus D

sim - ple words:_ O ma - kun - da o ma - kun - de.___ 1. May - be
smile and say___ O ma - kun - da o ma - kun - de.___ 2. May - be
...end solo) 3. May - be

Chorus:

F♯m7 Bm7 Bm7/A G A

we could learn___ to trust._ Si kou - da - li yet mat - su - re___
we could learn___ to share,_ Si kou - da - li yet mat - su - re___
we could learn___ to love,_ Si kou - da - li yet mat - su - re___

mf

Bm A/C♯ D A/C♯ Bm D/A

___ un - de.___ See the best in us.___ Si
___ un - de.___ As we dreamt one day,___ Si
___ un - de.___ As we dreamt one day,___ Si

1.
2.3.
G
A7sus
D
Bm7
kou - da - li yet mat - su - re.
dim.
Ta - ma -
Bridge:
F♯m7
F♯m/A
A
li yet mat - su - ra. Si kou - da - li yet mat - su - re
mf
Bm
A/C♯
D/A
un - de. Ta - ma - li yet ma. Si

To Coda
D.S. al Coda
G
Asus
D
kou - da - li yet mat - su - re.
dim.
Coda
D
Spread the
dim. poco a poco
mp
D2
word and say,
Kou - da - li o ma - kun - de.
D(9)
A/D
D(9)
p
pp

KUNYA SOBÉ

(from *Mystère Live*)

Music by
RENÉ DUPÉRÉ

8va
(8va)
(8va)
Kun -
ya So - bé ma-ni - é - vo sa - deil. Kun -

ya So - bé ma-ni - é - vo.
Yéké - sou-la mo-dié vo, yéké - sou-la sé-bo dié.
Yéké - sou-la mo-dié vo, yéké - sou-la sé-vié.
Yéké - sou-la mo-dié vo, yéké - sou-la sé-bo dié no.

Yéké - sou - la mo - dié vo,
yéké - sou - la sé - vié.
Em
C
D
Em
Cmaj7
Am7
Bm
Em
C
D
Em
Cmaj7
Am7
Bm
Em D/F♯

G Em C G Em Cmaj7 D G D/F♯
Em C D Em Cmaj7 Am7 Bm Em
C D Em Cmaj7 Am7 Bm Em
Kun - ya So - bé ma - ni - é - vo sa - deil.
C D Em Cmaj7 Am7 Bm Em D/F♯
Kun - ya So - bé ma - ni - é - vo.

G
Em
C
G
Em
Cmaj7
D
G
D/F♯
Kun - ya So - bé ma - ni - é - vo.
Em
C
D
Em
1.
Cmaj7
Am7
Bm
Em
Kun - ya So - bé ma - ni - é - vo sa - deil.
2.
Cmaj7
Am7
Bm
Em
D5
E5
ma - ni - é - vo sa - deil.

LET ME FALL

(from *Quidam*)

Lyrics by
JIM CORCORAN

Music by
BENOIT JUTRAS

Very slowly, with feeling (♩ = 66)

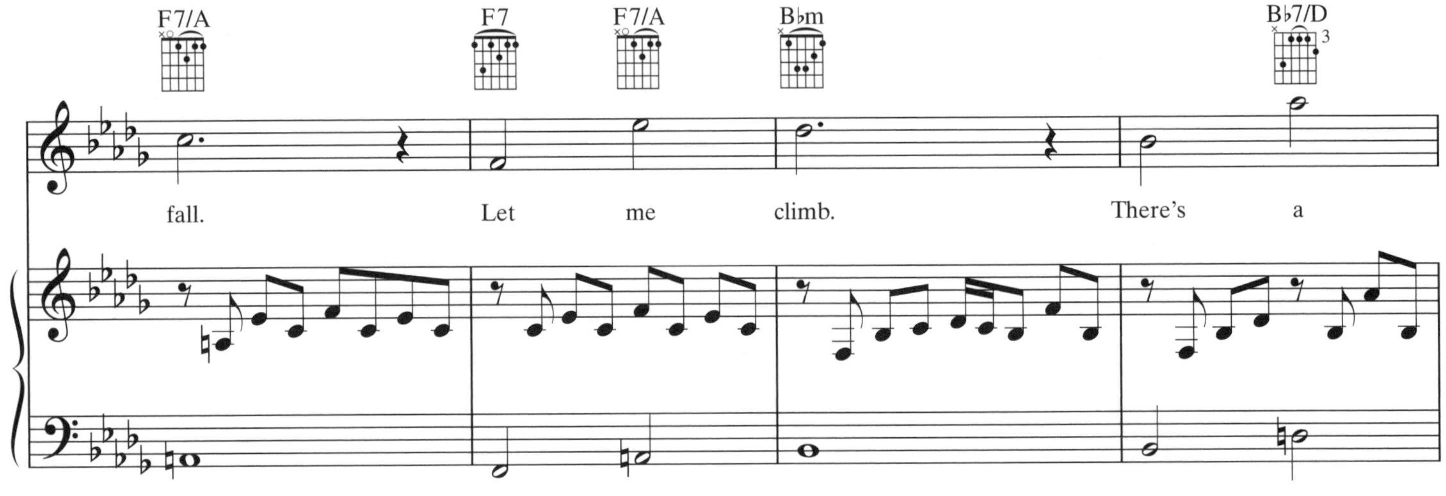

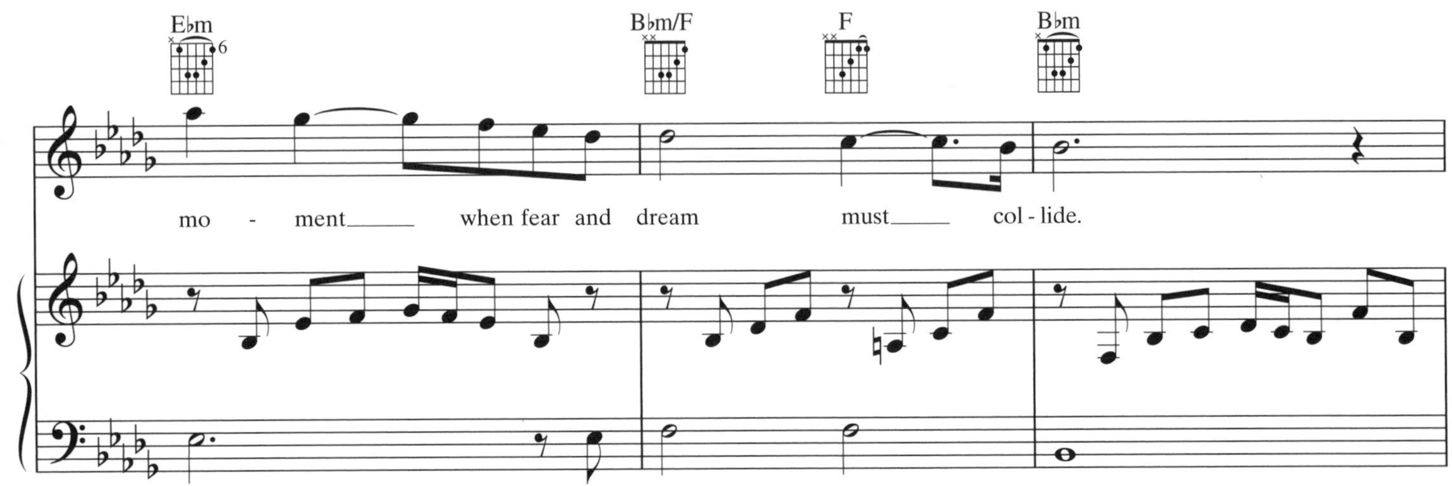

N.C.
B♭m/F
Some - one I am is wait - ing for cour - age. The one I
E♭m
E♭m/G♭
Edim7
G♭dim7
want, the one I will be-come will catch me. So
Am
E7
F
A7/C♯
Dm
Dm/F
let me fall if I must fall. I won't heed your warn - ings. I won't
Am/E
E
E7
Am
E7/G♯
hear them. All I ask,

E7
E7/G♯
Am
Am/C
A7/C♯
all I need, let me
Dsus
Dm
E♭dim7
E7sus
E7
o - pen which-ev - er door I might o - pen.
Am
E7/G♯
Am
E7/G♯
Am
Let me fall. If I fall,
Am/C
A7/C♯
Dsus
Dm
Am/E
E7
Am
though the phoe - nix may or may not rise.

A7
Dm
G7
I will dance so free - ly
hold - ing on to
Csus
C
E7
E7/G♯
Asus
Am
no one.
You can hold me on - ly if you
F(9)
C/E
Dm
Esus
E
too will fall a - way from all these use - less fears and chains.
Am
E7/G♯
E
E7/G♯
Oh,
oh,

Am
Am/C
A7/C♯
Dsus
Dm
oh,
Am/E
E7
F
F7
oh.
Oh,
some-one I
B♭m
F7
G♭
D♭
E♭m
E♭m/G♭
am is wait-ing for my cour-age.
The one I want, the one I will be-come will
Gdim7
Adim7
Am
E7
F
A7/C♯
catch me.
So let me fall if I must fall.
I won't heed your

Dm
Dm/F
Am/E
E7
warn - ings. I won't hear.
dim.
8vb
Am
E7/G♯
Am
E7/G♯
Let me fall. If I
mf
Am
Am/C
A7/C♯
Dsus
Dm
fall, there's no rea - son to miss this
Asus
Am
E7
E7sus(♭9)
E7(♭9)
Am
one chance, this per - fect mo - ment. Just let me fall.
rall.
mp
8vb

LIAMA
(from *La Nouba*)

Music by
BENOIT JUTRAS

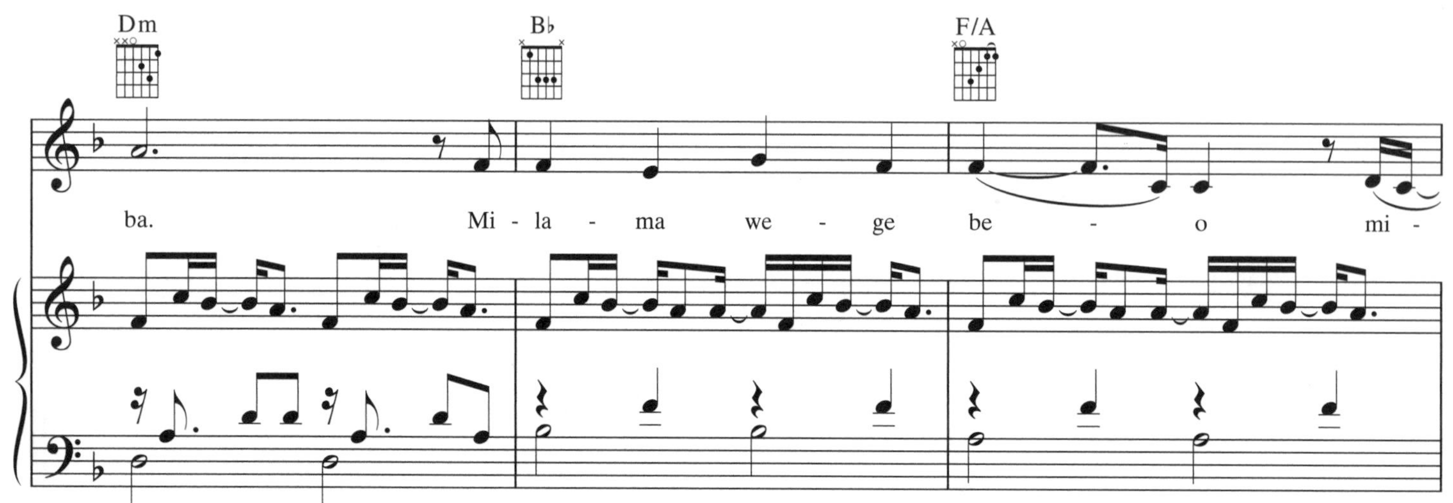

Csus
C
ma - ya - mo.
2. Mi -
Verse 2:
F
la - ma we - ge be - o, mi - la - ma we - gai
Dm
Am
B♭
F
ba. Si - vi - ah mi -
Csus
C
ma - ya - mo.

Chorus:
Dm
Csus
C
B♭
F/A
Am7
mf
Ma na za-vu - da_ ma-no__ me - ya, i-li__ li-
F
a - ma. Za - ku za-vi__ mi-en - du mi
To Coda
F(9)
zae li-a - ma wae. Ma na
za-vu - da_ ma-no__ me - ya, i-li__ li - a - ma.

Dm
Csus
C
B♭
F/A
B♭
Csus
C
Za - ku za-vi mi-en-du mi zae li-a-ma
F(9)
Dm
wae. Mi -
decresc.
mp
B♭(9)
la - ma we-ge be - o. Mi -
la - ma we - gai ba.
cresc.

Bridge:
Dm
Asus
B♭maj7
Dm/F
G2
Asus
B♭maj7
Dm/F
G2
Dm
Asus
mf
Oh,
yeah,
yeah.
Oh,
oh,
yeah,
oh.

Dm

mp

3. Mi -

Verse 3:

la - ma we - ge be - o, mi - la - ma we - gai

B♭(9) F/A

ba. Mi - la - ma we - ge be - o mi -

Csus C *D.S. 𝄋 al Coda*

ma - ya - mo.

Coda

F G Em Dsus D

wae. Ma na

C G/B Bm7 C G D

za-vu-da ma-no me-ya, i-li mi o - mo.

Em D C G/B

Za - ku za - bi mi - en - du mi

C Dsus D G(9)

zae li - a - ma wae.

MIO BELLO BELLO AMORE

(from *Zumanity, the Sensual Side of Cirque du Soleil*)

Lyrics by
ANNA LIANI

Music by
SIMON CARPENTIER

Mio Bello Bello Amore - 5 - 1

Verse 1:
Bm
Em7
Gmaj7
Gdim7
F♯
in - to you, so much to see in you. Can't get e - nough of your love. E - ven
(a tempo)
Freely
Bm
Em7
F♯7
here with you, I'm al - ways___ miss-ing you. Could it be bet - ter? Mi - o
Chorus:
Bm
Gmaj7
Gdim7
F♯
Bm
Bm/A
bel - lo, bel - lo, bel - lo a - mo - re, sei il mi - o pa - ra - di - so, when you
a tempo
G
A/G
A/C♯
D
A/E
F♯m
say I'm yours, when you ask me to stay. Si - a - mo

F#7
G#m7
F#/A#
so - li, so - li al mun - do. 2. I'll be
a tempo
Verse 2:
Bm
Em7
Gmaj7
Gdim7
F#
Bm
lov - ing you and kiss - ing your eyes, kiss - ing your smile. I'll be giv - ing you all that
Em7
F#7
Bm
F#/A#
I have good in - side. Mi - o
Chorus:
Bm
Gmaj7
F#
Em/B
Bm
bel - lo, bel - lo, bel - lo a - mo - re, sei il mi - o pa - ra - di - so, when you
a tempo

G
A
A/C♯
D
A/E
F♯m
say I'm yours, when you ask me to stay. Si - a - mo
F♯
To Coda
G♯m7
F♯/A♯
so - li, so - li al mun - do.
Bridge:
Bm
Gmaj7
F♯
Em/B
Bm
G
A
Na na na na na na na na na na na na
A/C♯
D
A/E
F♯m
F♯
na na na na na na. Mi-o
decresc.
l.h.

Chorus:
Bm
C♯m7(♭5)
F♯
Bm
G
Em/G
bel-lo, bel-lo, bel-lo a - mo-re, sei il mi-o pa-ra - di-so, quan-do di - ci so-no tu - a, quan-do
mp
A/C♯ D A/E F♯m
F♯
D.S. 𝄋 al Coda
G♯m7 F♯/A♯
mi vuoi con te. Si - a-mo so - li, so-li al - mun-do. Mi-o
rit.
Coda
Freely
Bm
mun - do. Mi - o bel - lo, bel - lo, bel - lo a -
mp
Gmaj7
F♯
Bm
mo - re, bel - lo a - mo - re.

LOVE DANCE

(from *KÀ*)

Music by
RENÉ DUPÉRÉ

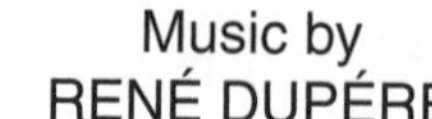

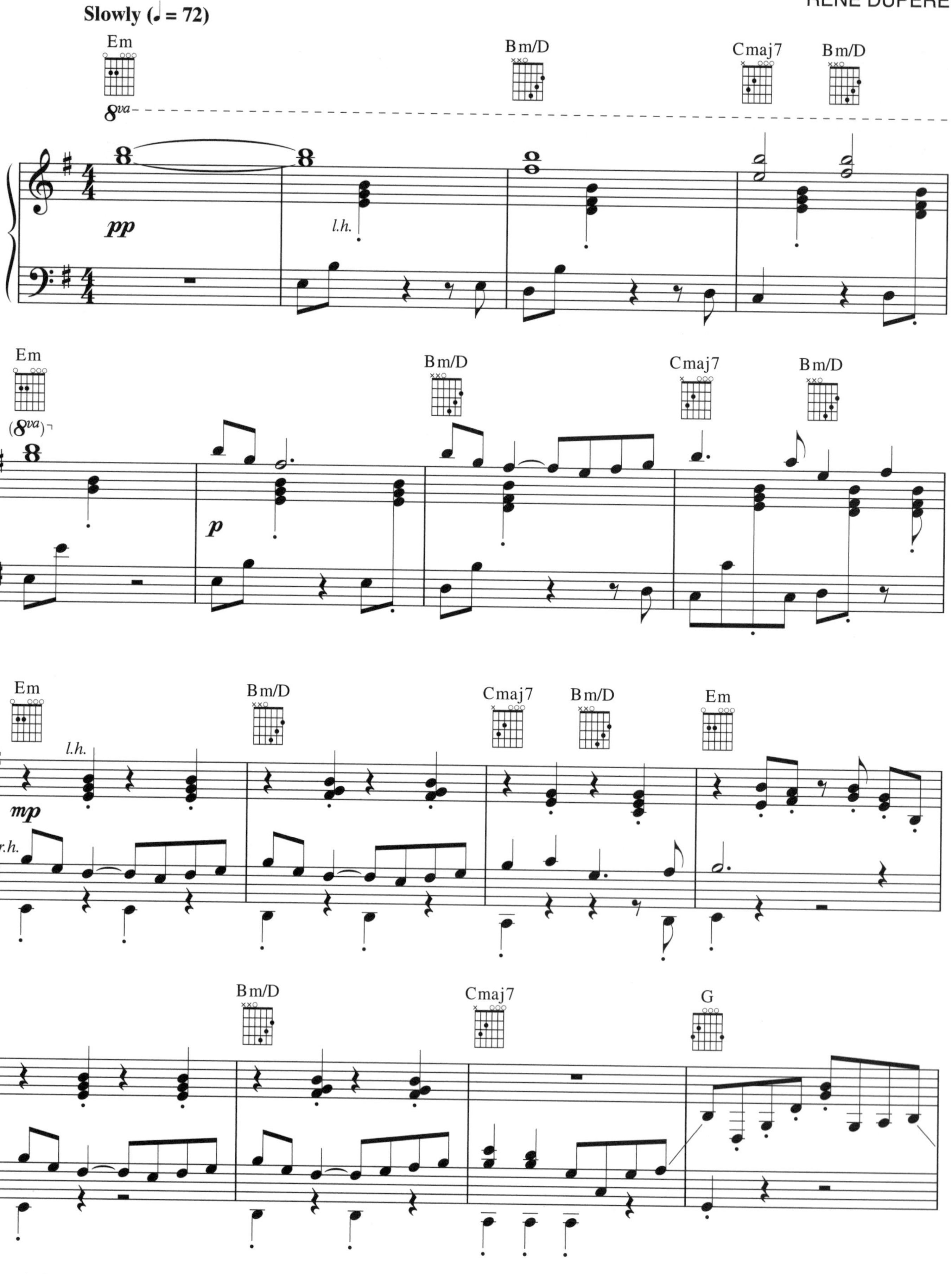
Slowly (♩ = 72)
Em
Bm/D
Cmaj7
Bm/D
8va
pp
l.h.
Em
Bm/D
Cmaj7
Bm/D
(8va)
p
Em
Bm/D
Cmaj7
Bm/D
Em
l.h.
mp
r.h.
Bm/D
Cmaj7
G

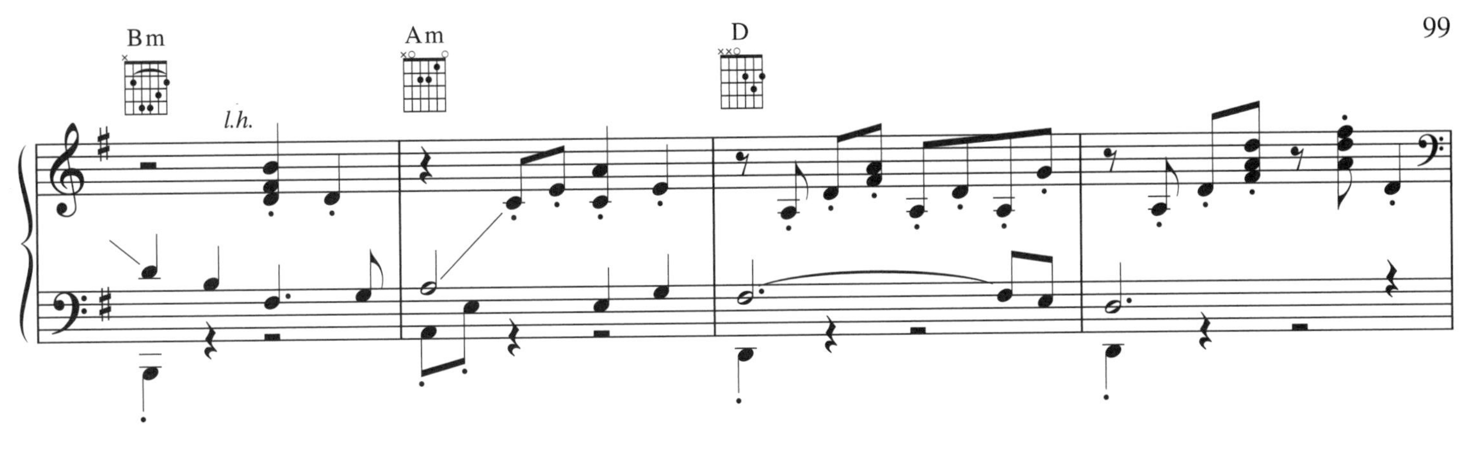
Bm
Am
D
l.h.

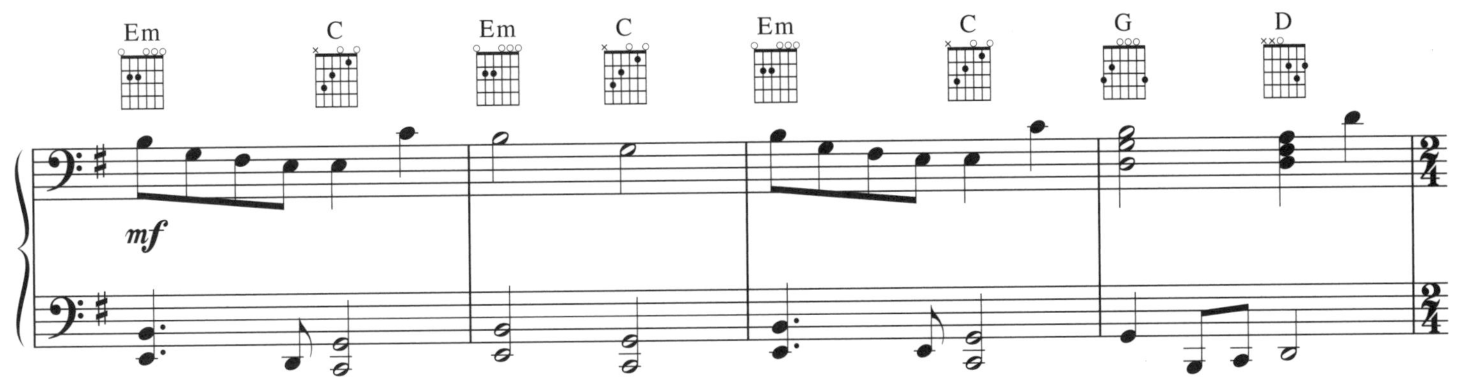
Em
C
Em
C
Em
C
G
D
mf

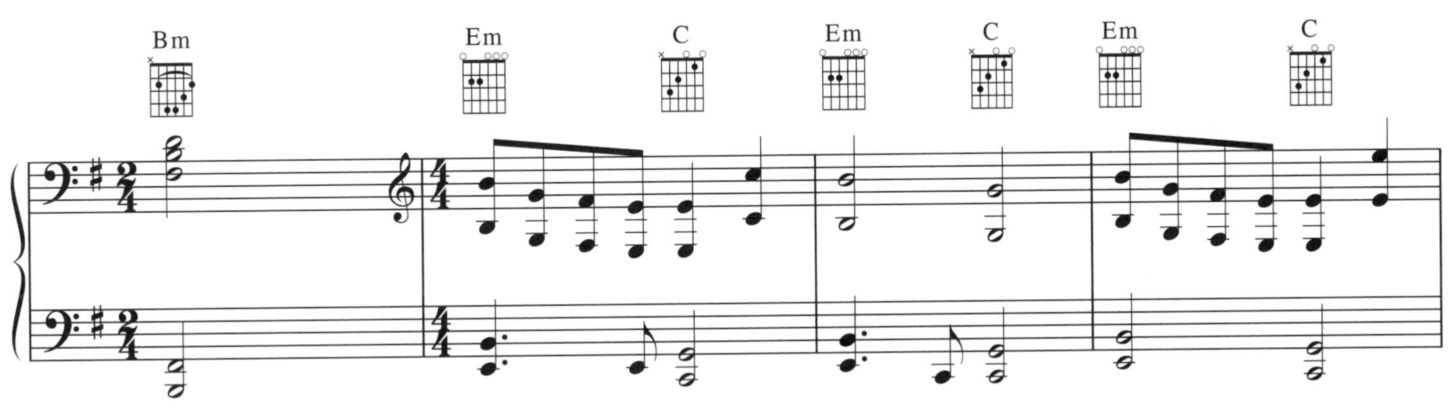
Bm
Em
C
Em
C
Em
C

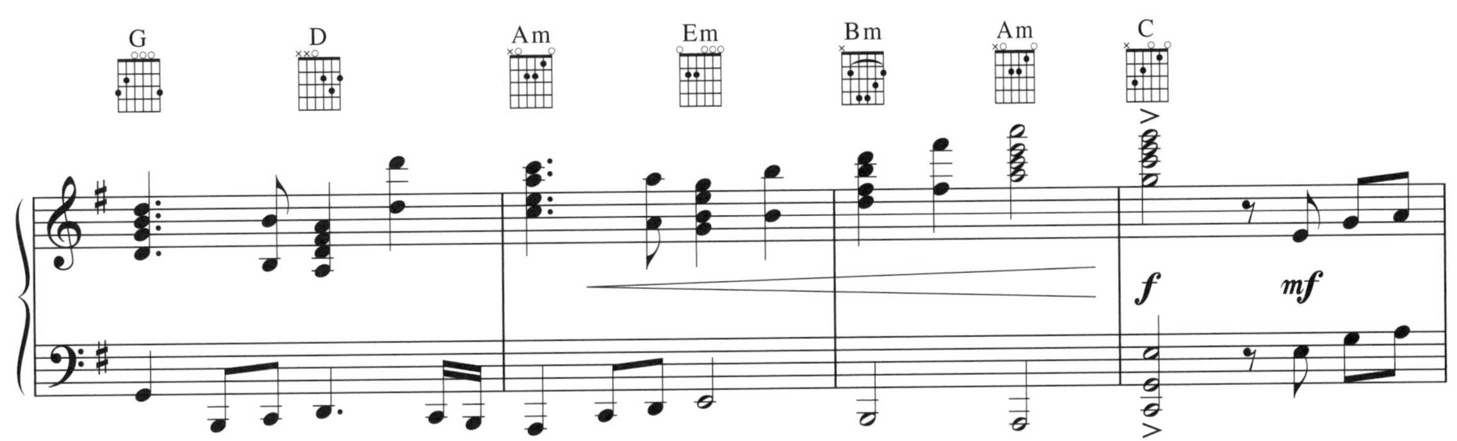
G
D
Am
Em
Bm
Am
C
f
mf

Broadly
Em
C
G
D
Am
Em
Bsus
f
F♯m
D
A
E
B
F♯m
D
Dm
E
Misterioso
Am
Em/G
D/F♯
E/G♯
Am
Em/G
mf
D/F♯
E/G♯
Am
Em/G
D/F♯
E/G♯
Boy Soprano:
Oh.

Am
Em/G
D/F♯
E/G♯
Am
Em/G
D/F♯
E/G♯
Oh.
Oh.
F♯m
E/F♯
F♯m
E/F♯
F♯m
Oh.
Oh.
8va
mp
E/F♯
F♯m
(8va)
p
dim.
pp
rit.

NOSTALGIE

(from «O»)

Music by
BENOIT JUTRAS

Dm(9)
Em(9)
Am(9)
Bm(9)
yun ya - crun - ya es tal - yo. Sve - gal - ya
Bm7(♭5)
C♯m7(♭5)
E
F♯
Am
Bm
de - ne gra - col - ya se - cu - ya. Son - yo es
cresc.
Chorus:
A
B
Dm(9)
Em(9)
cun - yo. Cri yo es tan - yu. Ne ya - ka
2. (Instrumental solo cont....
mp
Bm7(♭5)
C♯m7(♭5)
E7
F♯7
Am(9)
Bm(9)
so - ye. Tu - si cri - o con - ye tu - lu. Smo di es
dim.

Dm(9)
Em(9)
su - va, cal - yo es ya - bo. Sve - dal - ya
Bdim
C♯dim
E
F♯
1.
Am(9)
Bm(9)
co es to ya-crun-ya svi ja - bo. Son - yo es
2.
Am(9)
Bm(9)
bo.
D.S. 𝄋
3.
Am(9)
Bm(9)
D.S. 𝄋
...end solo) 3. Smo__ di es
4.
Am(9)
Bm(9)
bo.
dim.

OMÉ YO KANOUBÉ

(from *TOTEM*)

Music by
BOB & BILL
(GUY DUBUC and MARC LESSARD)

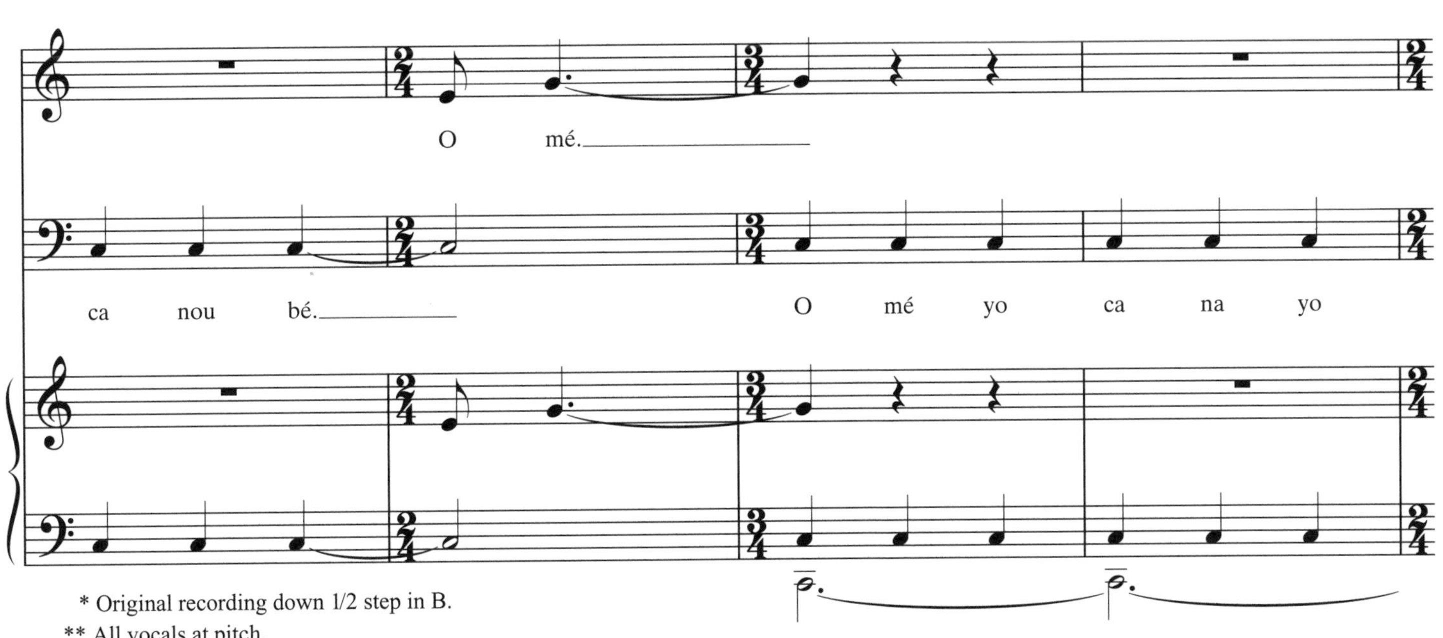

* Original recording down 1/2 step in B.
** All vocals at pitch.

djé so o mé yo ca nou bé.
O mé yo ca na yo djé so o mé yo
ca nou bé.
O mé yo ca na yo
O mé yo ca na yo

djé so o mé yo ca nou bé.
djé so o mé yo ca nou bé.
O mé yo ca na yo djé so
O mé yo ca no yo djé so
O mé yo ca na yo djé so
o mé yo ca nou bé. O mé.
o mé yo ca nou bé.
o mé yo ca nou bé.

O mé yo ca na yo djé so
o mé yo ca nou bé.
Moderately ♩ = 104
O mé,
o mé yo ka nou bé,

ka ne ka na yo djé so no ka wé.
O mé,
o mé yo
ka na yo ka nu bé.
C
F
Ton gné gné gné gné gné gné ton - gué,
ton - pa a *ton gué par da.*
C
F
Ton gné gné gné gné gné gné ton - gué,
ton - pa a *ton gué par da.*

C
G
Zig - gy pa - té, zig - gy pa, zig - gy pa - té a ton gué pa.
C
Ton gné gné gné gné gné gné ton - gué, zig - gy pa - té, a ton qué pa.
O mé,
F
o mé yo ka nou bé,
C
F
ka ne ka na yo djé so ka wé.
O mé,

C F N.C.

o mé yo ka na yo ka nu bé. O mé,

D

o mé yo ka nou bé,

ka ne ka na yo djé so ka wé. O mé,

Bm7 A7

o mé yo ka na yo ka nu bé.

D
1.
2.
O mé,
N.C.
D/F♯
G
O mé yo ka nou bé. O mé yo
D
ka nou bé. O mé yo ka nou bé.

Gm/B♭
G2
O mé yo ka nou bé. O mé yo
D
ka nou bé. O mé, o mé yo ka nou bé,
ka ne ka na yo djé so ka wé. O mé,
Bm7
A7
D
o mé yo ka na yo ka nu bé.

O

(from «O»)

Music by
BENOIT JUTRAS

O - 2 - 1

D
A/C♯
Bm
A6
G
D/A
A
D
A/C♯
Bm
A6
G
D/A
A
F♯m
G
Em
F♯sus
F♯
Bm
Gmaj7
D/A
A
D
A/C♯
Bm
A6
Gmaj7
Asus
A
Bm
Bm/A
Gmaj7
Asus
A
D
p

OMBRA
(from *Dralion*)

Lyrics by
HÉLÈNE DORION

Music by
VIOLAINE CORRADI

E♭maj7
B♭maj7/F
Il sen - tie - ro è là, è là e al di
Gm(9)
là.
1. Al -
Gsus
lo - ra vien - ne l' - al - ba. Co - me si
Gsus2 sus4
Gm(9)
dà il fio - re al so - le. Il tem - po

E♭maj7
B♭maj7/F
sem - pre vol - ge - ra
È il nos - tro
Gm(9)
viag - gio.
Co - sì,
cresc.
Gm
Cm6
il mon - do si al - za, u - no
mf
Gm
vi - so s'il - lum - i - na.
Il tem - po

Ebmaj7
F
sem - pre vol - ge - ra
È il nos - tro
(Spoken:) Une éternité... ...cerclée de poussière..., ...perce l'éphémère.
Interlude:
Gm
Ab/G
viag - gio.
Ebmaj7
Bbmaj7/F
Gm(9)
dim.

Gm(9)
Gsus
Om - bra, om - brel - li - no, sot - to
mp
Gsus2 sus4
Gm(9)
L'ar - co del cie - lo.
E♭maj7
B♭maj7/F
Il sen - tie - ro è là, è là e al di
Gm(9)
là.
(Inst. solo …

Gsus
Gsus2 sus4
Gm(9)
…end solo)
Il tem - po
E♭maj7
B♭maj7/F
sem - pre vol - ge - ra
È il nos - tro
(Spoken:) Une éternité… …cerclée de poussière…, …perce l'éphémère.
Gm(9)
viag - gio.
All
mf

Gsus
Gsus2 sus4
winds and tides, sand and
Gm(9)
Ebmaj7
si - lence. O - ver the
Bbmaj7/F
G
G7sus
Ab/G
dis - tance slip - ping through our hands.
To Coda
(Instrumental fills)

Interlude:
Fm(9)
mf
Db
4
Eb
Fm(9)
Db
4
Eb
3
3
3
3
3

Gm
Cm6
La gio - ia ci ri - ve - la - no. Co - me si
mf
Gm
dà il fio - re al so - le. Il tem - po
3
E♭maj7
F
sem - pre vol - ge - ra È il nos - tro
(Spoken:) Des jours fragiles... ...et nuits sans défense,... ...la roue tournero.
Gm
Cm6
viag - gio.

Gm
E♭maj7
Il tem-po sem - pre vol-ge-ra
(Spoken:) Des jours fragiles...
F
Gm
D.S. 𝄋 al Coda
È il nos - tro viag - gio.
...et nuits sans défense,... ...la roue tournero.
⊕ Coda
G
G7sus
A♭/G
(Instrumental fills cont.)
dim. poco a poco
Repeat 3 times
p

PAGEANT

(from *KÀ*)

Music by
RENÉ DUPÉRÉ

Dm
Am
Dm
Am
Dm
Am
Dm
Dm
Am
Dm
Am
Dm
Am
Staa - va hoy-na-re - a va staa - va, hosh-ta may-hie ma mil - ya, hoy-na-re - a va
mf
Dm
Am
Dm
Am
Dm
Am
staa - va. Hosh-ta may-hie ma mil - ya, hat-sum ga-ra kum ja - ra, hat-sum mo-ra is -

Dm
Am
Dm
Am
Em
taa - va, hat-sum me-ra ie chel - la. Sta-vum mie-ra ien ja - ra, ha-ya mi-ea va
Am
Em
Am
Em
Am
Em
staa - va, hosh-ta may-hie ma mil - ya sta-vum me-ra ien ja - ra, hoy-na-re-a va
F
C
Dm
Am
B♭
F
staa - va, hat-sum ga-ra kum ja - ra, hat-sum mo-ra is - taa - va, hat-sum me-ra ie
G
1.
2.
chel - la.

A
Dm
C/E
Staa - va.
Ahh.
F
G
Dm
A
B♭
F
Gm
A
Ahh.
Dm
G
1.
Dm
Asus
A
2.
Dm/A
A
Dm
C/E
F
G
Dm
A
B♭
F
Ahh.
Ahh.

Gm
A
Dm
G
Dm
G
A
cresc.
Dm
C/E
F
G
Dm
A
B♭
F
Ahh.
Ahh.
Gm
A
1.
Dm
Gm
Dm/A
A7
Ahh.
2.
Dm
Gm
Dm/A
A7
Dm
Ahh.

PEARL

(from *KOOZA*)

Music by
JEAN-FRANÇOIS CÔTÉ

Moderately, in "1" 𝅗𝅥. = 54 (♩ = 162)

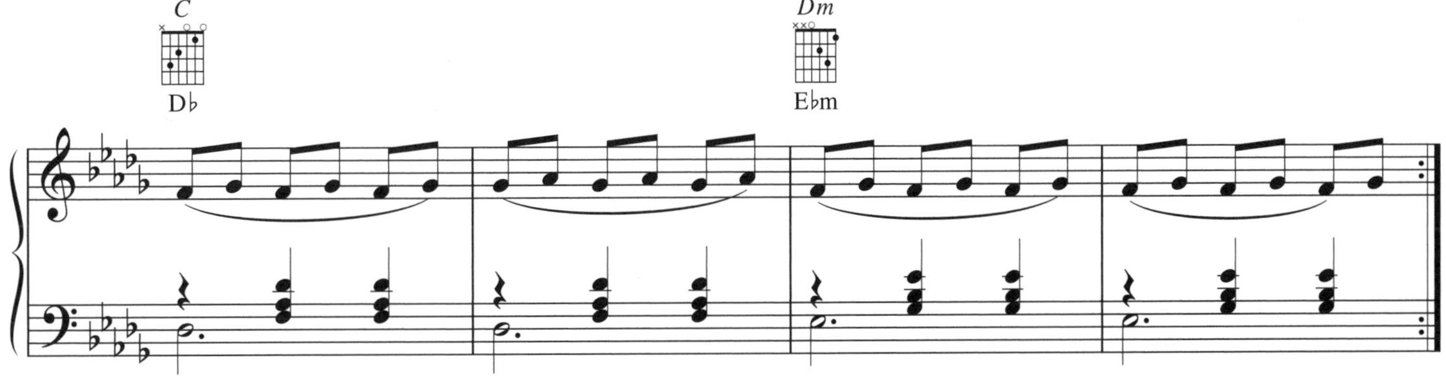

Verse:
Am
B♭m
A♭dim7
Adim7
Don se la - vi - don son - toi - no
C
D♭
Dm
E♭m
e - se - la di - non son no. De -
E
F
Am
B♭m
he - la da vi - da mon - se -
B
C
E
F
dou, he se - no.

Am
B♭m
A♭dim7
Adim7
Don se la-don-vi dou-si-na
C
D♭
Dm
E♭m
De-ne-sa ha noo-son-koa. De-
E
F
Am
B♭m
B
C
he-la da vi-da mon-se-dou,
E
F
E/F♯
F/G
E/G♯
F/A
E
F
he se-no.

Chorus:
Dm
E♭m
Dm/C
E♭m/D♭
Bm7(♭5)
Cm7(♭5)
Am/E
B♭m/F
(Ooh)
Ha - la - ve, Ha - la -
Am
B♭m
Am/G
B♭m/A♭
D/F♯
E♭/G
Fdim7
G♭dim7
van. Don - se - koa he non - ce
A♭dim7
Adim7
Am
B♭m
Bdim7
Cdim7
C
D♭
no - si - son - toi.
Dm
E♭m
C
D♭
Dm
E♭m
Do - ce - la -

Am
A♭dim7
Am
D/F♯
B♭m
Adim7
B♭m
E♭/G
vi, do - te - la - nui.
Bo - te - la -
G
A♭dim7
Am
A♭
Adim7
B♭m
Do - ce - la - nui, do - ble
vi, ob - li le - son. He - se -
D/F♯
G
To Coda
E♭/G
A♭
la - sone nou - sa -
toi ni no - va
Am
A♭dim7
B♭m
Adim7
le.

C
D♭
Dm
E♭m
Am
B♭m
Wa
ah
A♭dim7
Adim7
ah
C
D♭
Dm
E♭m
wa
ah.
Am
B♭m
Am/G♯
B♭m/A
D.S. 𝄋 al Coda

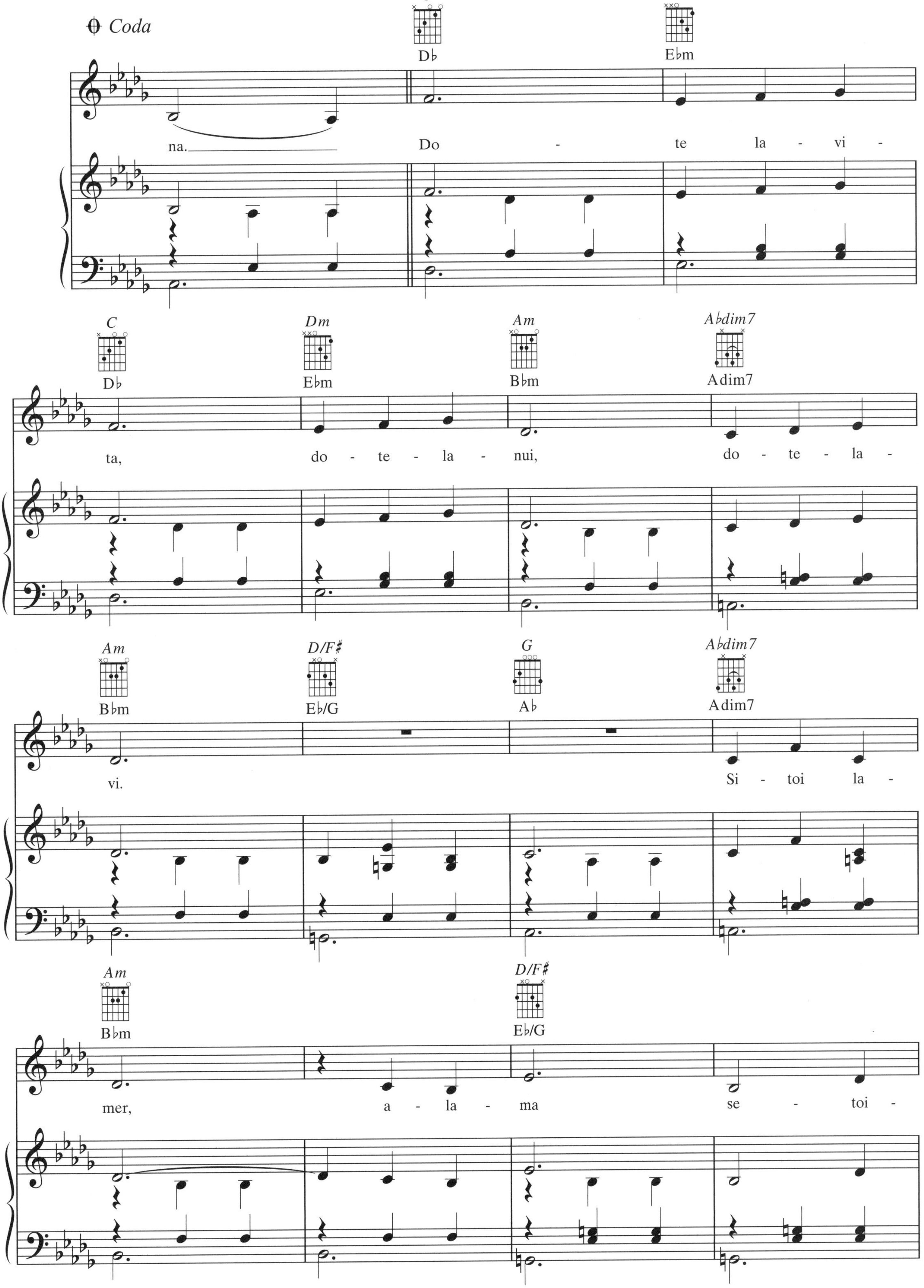

𝄌 *Coda*

C / D♭ — *Dm* / E♭m

na. Do - te la - vi -

C / D♭ — *Dm* / E♭m — *Am* / B♭m — *A♭dim7* / Adim7

ta, do - te - la - nui, do - te - la -

Am / B♭m — *D/F♯* / E♭/G — *G* / A♭ — *A♭dim7* / Adim7

vi. Si - toi la -

Am / B♭m — *D/F♯* / E♭/G

mer, a - la - ma se - toi -

G
A♭
A♭dim7
Adim7
le.
Am
B♭m
B♭
B
Am
B♭m
B♭
B
Am
B♭m
B♭
B
Am
B♭m
E
F
Am
B♭m
B♭
B
Am
B♭m
B♭
B

Am Bb Am E
Bbm B Bbm F

Dm Dm/C Bm7(b5)
Ebm Ebm/Db Cm7(b5)

Ha - la -

Am/E Am Am/G D/F#
Bbm/F Bbm Bbm/Ab Eb/G

ve, Ha - le - van. Don - se - koa he

F Am
Gb Bbm

non - ce.

QUÉ VIYÉRA
(from *TOTEM*)

Music by
BOB & BILL
(GUY DUBUC and MARC LESSARD)

Cm Ebm

F#m

Am N.C.

Cm Bb6 Bb Ab6 Ab G

Cm Bb6 Bb Ab6 Ab G

Cm
Bb6
Bb
Ab6
Ab
Que, vi ye - ra pe - ra yo el - fi -
G
Cm
Bb6
Bb
na kun te di - o. Vi ye ra mi da
Ab6
Ab
G
Cm
sion pe - ra yo cor - i - zon. Ma - si
Bb6
Bb
Ab6
Ab
G
le ye sel a - vor es pour a - ye cor - i -

Cm
B♭6
B♭
A♭6
A♭
zon. Vi - ye - ra pe - ra yo, al - fi
G
Fm
A♭maj7
na kun te un da.
Cm
B♭
Fm
A♭maj7
Cm
B♭

Dm
F
B♭
Que, vi ye - ra pe - ra yo el - fi -
A
Dm
F
na kun te dio. Vi - ye - ra mi - da -
B♭
A
Cm
3
sion pe - ra yo... El do
B♭/D
E♭maj7
B♭/F
so que tel pie - ra en fi na ves - ti

Eb/G
Ab
Dm7(b5)
yo. En van do que tel pie - ra ves - ti
G
Cm
Bb
yo es quie - ran - da...
Ab
G7
Fm
Fm/Eb
Dm7(b5)
N.C.

Cm
B♭
a tempo
A♭
G
Cm
B♭
A♭
G

Cm
B♭/D
E♭
El do so que tel pie-ra en fi
B♭/F
Gm
A♭
na ves - ti yo. En van do que tel
Dm7(♭5)
G
Cm
pie-ra ves - ti yo es quie - ran - da...
E♭m
F♯m

Am
N.C.
Guitar ad lib.
Cm
B♭6
B♭
A♭6
A♭
G
Cm
B♭6
B♭
A♭6
A♭
G
Cm
B♭6
B♭
A♭6
A♭
G
Vocal ad lib.
Cm
B♭/D
E♭

B♭/F
Gm
A♭
Dm7(♭5)
G
Cm
E♭m
F♯m
Am
N.C.

QUERER
(from *Alegría*)

Lyrics by
MANUEL TADROS

Music by
RENÉ DUPÉRÉ

Dm F♯dim7 Gm B♭/F Em7(♭5) A7
zón con el fue-go de la pa-sión. Que-
dad sen-ti-mien-to de li-ber-tad. Que-
Dm A7sus Dm A7sus
rer, sin mi-rar hacia atras a tra-ves de los
rer, sin jamas es-pe-rar dar so-lo pa-ra
Dm F♯m D/F♯ Gm F
o-jos si-em-pre y to-da-vi-a mas.
dar si-em-pre y to-da-vi-a mas.
1.2. A-
Chorus:
B♭ C/B♭ Am7 Dm F
mar, pa-ra po-dar lu-char, con-tra el vien-to y vo-
3. (Inst. solo ad lib.…

Gm
Gm7
C7
Fmaj7
B♭maj7
E7sus
A7
lar, des - cu-brir la be - lle - za del mar. Que -
Dm
A7sus
Dm
A7
rer, y po - der com-par - tir nues - tra sed de vi -
Dm
F♯dim7
Gm
B♭/F
Em7(♭5)
A7
vir. El re - ga - lo que nos da el a - mor, es la
1.
2.
D.S. 𝄋
Dm
A7sus
Dm
Dm/C
vi - da. vi - da.

3.
Dm
A7sus
Dm
A7sus
vi - da.
Dm
A7sus
Dm
F♯dim7
Gm
B♭/F
Em7(♭5)
A7
Dm
B♭
Gm6
Dm/A
A7sus
Dm
B♭
Gm6
Dm/A
A7sus
A7
Dm

QUIDAM
(from *Quidam*)

Lyrics by
JIM CORCORAN

Music by
BENOIT JUTRAS

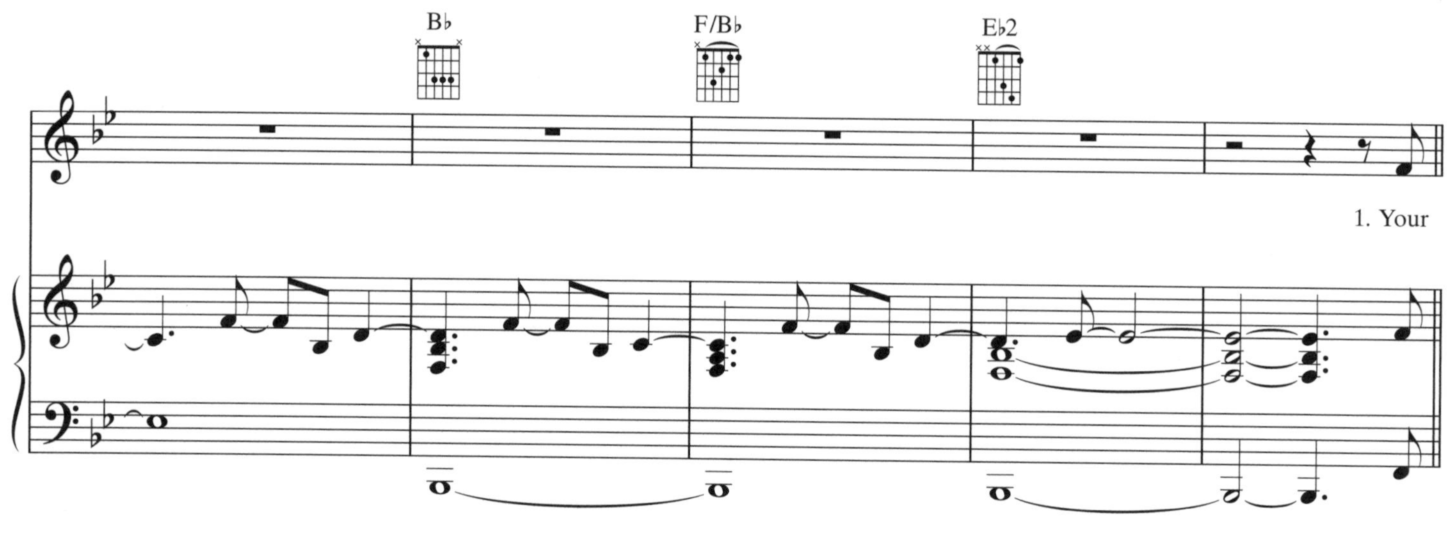

B♭(9)
F/B♭
E♭9
may have touched the stars, but they weren't moved.
B♭(9)
F/B♭
And if you reach for me, I may not
Gm
E♭
B♭(9)
F/B♭
choose to hold your hand. I might smile, or I might turn a-
E♭9
D7/F♯
Gm
way. An or-di-nar-y man, Qui-dam. I'm

Cm7
Cm7/F
ev - 'ry man. I'm an - y man. Qui - dam,
Chorus:
B♭/D
F(9)
Gm7
E♭9
Qui - dam, la nuit re - cule. D'un rêve
mf
B♭/D
F(9)
Gm7
E♭2
à l'autre tu valses. Du creux
B♭(9)
F(9)
Gm7
E♭9
de toi c'est bien la mal qui dres-

B♭/D
F(9)
Gm7
E♭2
se tes
si - lences.
2. There's
Verse 2:
B♭(9)/D
F
E♭2
noth-ing left,
there's noth-ing right,
there's noth-ing wrong.
I'm
B♭(9)/D
F
E♭9
one, I'm two,
I'm all
yet none of you.
The
B♭(9)
F
Gm
E♭
truth, the lie,
the tear,
the laugh - ter,
the hand and the emp-ty touch.
Here I am

B♭(9)/D
F
E♭(9)
a - lone, wait - ing for the cur-tain call. An
D7/F♯
Gm
Cm7
or - di - nar - y man, Qui - dam. I'm ev - 'ry man.
(T'es
Cm7/F
I'm an - y man. Qui - dam,
l'in - con - nu.) (T'es l'é - tran - ger.)
Chorus:
B♭/E♭
F(9)
Gm7
E♭2
Qui - dam, la nuit re - cule. D'un rêve
mf

B♭/D
F(9)
Gm7
E♭2
à l'autre
tu valses.
Du creux
B♭(9)
F(9)
Gm7
E♭2
de toi
c'est bien
la mal
qui dres-
To Coda
B♭/E♭
F(9)
Gm7
E♭2
se tes
si - lences.
Bridge:
F
D7
Gm
Gm/F
Bai - lo en es - te lien - zo de do - lor.
Fu -

E♭
E♭m
B♭
nàm - bu - lo sin ma - pa ni brù - ju - la.
La
F
D7
E♭
E♭m
dul - ce lo - cu - ra mi sò - lo re - fu - gio.
Naz - co en la
B♭
F
D.S. 𝄋 al Coda
som - bra del pa - ya - so.
Qui - dam,
⊕ Coda
Gm7
E♭2
Qui - dam,

Chorus:
C
G
Am7
F(9)
Qui - dam,
aux rives
la nuit
du rêves.
re - cule.
Au seuil
D'un rêve
de l'ombre,
à l'autre
tu valses.
tu valses.
Au - tour
Du creux
de toi
c'est bien
la mal
qui dres-
se tes
si - lences.
Qui - dam,
Repeat ad lib. and fade

SOLITUDE

(from *KOOZA*)

Music by
JEAN-FRANÇOIS CÔTÉ

Moderately slow ♩ = 84

Bm7
A/C♯
D
Asus/E
D
D/F♯
G(9)
Asus
Bm7
Asus
G2
A
N.C.
D
Asus/C♯
G/B

*Lyrics represent non-translating syllables.

ba da boo bi de eh ba da boo ba da boo ba da boo ba da boo ba da boo ba da.
D
A/C♯
G/B
A/C♯
D
A/C♯
G/B
G
D/F♯
Em
D
A/C♯
Em
D
A/C♯
D
D/F♯

G2
Asus
Bm7
A/C♯
D
Asus/E
Double-time feel (♩ = ♩)
D
Asus/C♯
G/B
Asus/C♯
D
Asus/C♯
Ti do
off do a bre
G/B
Asus/C♯
D
eh a bre eh beh do.
Ti do

Asus/C♯
G/B
Asus/C♯
off do a bre eh a bre eh bea de.
Original feel
N.C.
D

TIME FLIES
(from *DELIRIUM*)

Lyrics by
ROBERT DILLON

Music by
BENOIT JUTRAS
Arrangement by
FRANCIS COLLARD

Moderately fast dance feel ♩ = 128

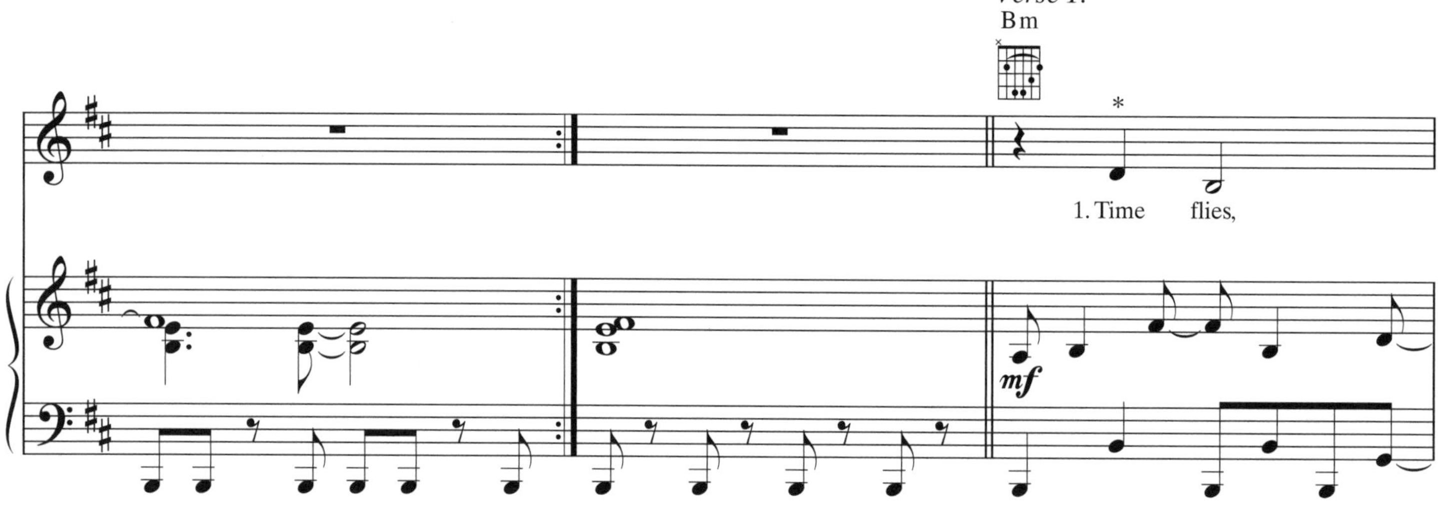

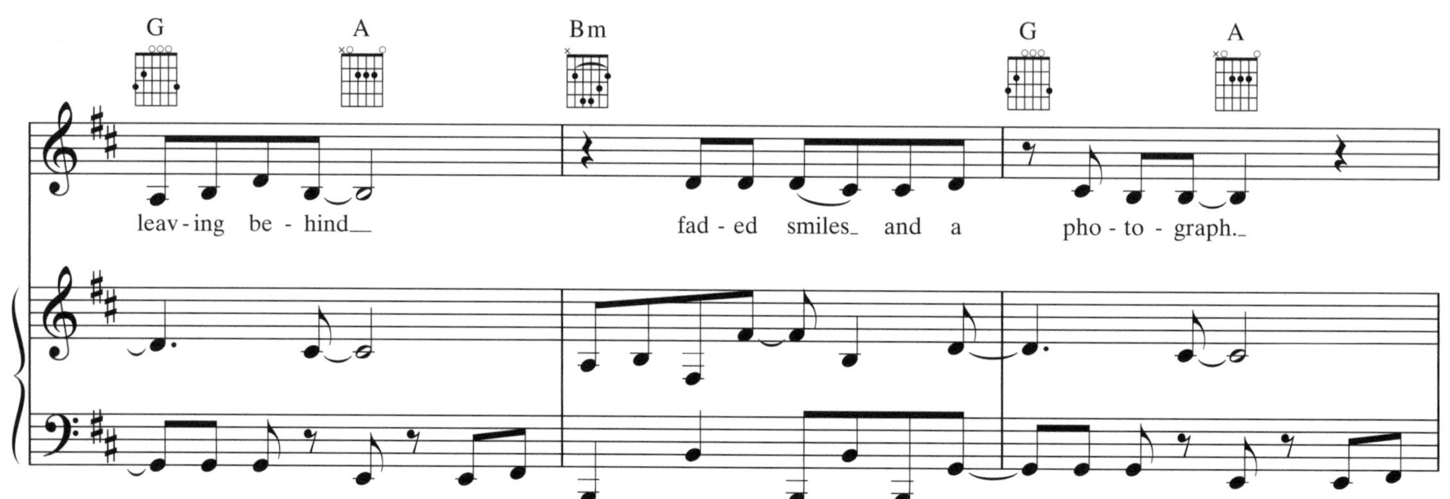

*All vocals written at pitch.

Bm
G
A
Bm
Clocks chime, sec-onds un - wind,
pre-cious mo-ments slip-ping
Verse 2:
G
A
Bm
G
A
in - to the past.
2. Time flies,
push-ing for - ward and all
Bm
G
A
Bm
we are will one day pass.
Move on but
G
A
Bm
G
A
don't ig - nore the shad - ows in the look - ing glass.

Chorus:
Bm
G
A
Bm
Old friends, lov - ers and oth - ers, don't know when I'll see you a - gain.
G
A
Bm
G
A
Time flies, soon - er or lat - er, our sto -
Bm
G
A
Verse 3:
Bm
ry must come to an end.
3. All I know
G
A
Bm
G
A
is we em - bark on sep - 'rate jour - neys. Wher - ev - er I go,

Bm
G
A
Bm
G
A
__ you're al - ways with__ me. Ev-'ry end - ing is__ a new__ be - gin - ning.
B2
Es -
Bridge:
Bm
A
G
D/F♯
now__ je goi - lia ku, im -
Em
Bm
B2
F♯sus
D♯sus
D♯
be - ia - nee, la sol - yae gos - na

G♯sus
G♯
F♯dim7
G♯
vem - bra. May dra - jay le
C♯m
Bdim7
swa - la - nee. Zy - niem - bo, sae gra -
F♯m
F
Am/E
ur - ni - as nye. Je - pan -
D♯dim7
B7
Em
B7
Em
ia cris - tu - ian man - do. Le - si -

Am
Em/G
Fmaj7
C/E
ae,
je
goi
-
lia
-
ku,
im
-
Dm7
C
Dm7
Esus
E
be
-
ia
-
nee,
et
may
C5
B(9)
yae.
Chorus:
Bm
G
A
Bm
Time flies,
tak - ing us far - ther from fac - es and plac - es we know.

G
A
Bm
G
A
Time flies,
al - ways re - mem - ber you're with
Bm
G
A
Bm
me wher - ev - er I go.
Old friends,
G
A
Bm
G
A
lov - ers and oth - ers, don't know when I'll see you a - gain.
Bm
G
A
Bm
To Coda
Time flies,
soon - er or lat - er, our sto - ry must come to an end.

1.
2.
G
A
Bm
G
A
Bm
G
A
D.S. 𝄋 al Coda
Bm
G
A
Bm
G
A
𝄌 Coda
G
A
Bm

TRIANGLE TANGO

(from *Corteo*)

Music by
PHILIPPE LEDUC

F♯7(♯5)
C♯m7(♭5)
Em6
F♯7
accel.
L.H.
rubato
G7(♭9)
8va
R.H.
L.H.
accel.
ff
Moderate tango (♩ = 116)
Cm
A♭7
G7
Cm
Fm
mf
Dm7(♭5)
G7
A♭
D7(♯9)
G

Cm
A♭7
G7
Cm
Fm
Dm7(♭5)
G7
A♭
D7(♯9)
G7
Fm
Fm6/A♭
G7
A♭7/G♭
G7
Cm
Fm
Dm7(♭5)
G7
B♭/A♭
A♭
D7(♭9)
D7(♯9)
G7

Cm
Fm
Dm7(♭5)
G7
A♭
F♯dim7
G7
Cm
Cm
Cm7
Cm6
Fm
Ya ya da ya da da ya da ya ya. Ya ya da da da da ya da ya da.
Dm7(♭5)
G7
Dm7(♭5)
1. G7
2. A♭
G
A♭7
G7
C7(♯5)
Fm

C7(♯5)
Fm
Cm7(♭5)
F7
B♭m
F7
B♭m
Cm7(♭5)
F7
B♭m
Gm7
G♭7
cresc.
F7(♭5)
A♭7
G7
A♭7
G7
Cm
A♭7
G7
f
mf
Cm
Fm

Dm7(♭5)
G7
B♭/A♭
A♭
D7(♭9)
G
Cm
Cdim/G
G7
Cm
Fm
Dm7(♭5)
G
A♭
F♯dim7
G7
Cm
Dm7(♭5)
G7
cresc.
f
A♭
F♯dim7
G7
Cm
N.C.

POKINOÏ

(from *Saltimbanco*)

Music by
RENÉ DUPÉRÉ

Gm7
Am7
Dm
Dsus2 sus4
Dm
Os - ti-nyi du brach ti-vo.
Gm7
Am7
B♭
Dm/F
Po - ki-noï, Po-ki-noï dji noch pre - do.
Gm7
Am7
Dm
Dsus2 sus4
Dm
Os - ti-nyi du brach ti-vo.
Dm
Dsus2 sus4
Dm
Dsus2 sus4
Dm

Verse:
Dm
D sus2 sus4
Po - ki - noï dji noch pre - do.
Os - ti - nyi du brach ti - vo.
Va - ga-na - i tu maj - ga - di.
To Coda
Ich ka - ra ku dar - ta nyi.

Chorus:

Gm7 Am7 B♭ Dm/F

Po - ki - noï, Po - ki - noï dji noch pre - do.

Gm7 Am7 Dm D sus2 sus4 Dm

Os - ti - nyi du brach ti - vo.

Gm7 Am7 B♭ Dm/F

Po - ki - noï, Po - ki - noï dji noch pre - do.

Gm7 Am7 Dm D sus2 sus4 Dm

Os - ti - nyi du brach ti - vo.

Dm(9)
Po - ki - noï,
Po - ki - noï.
Accordion solo:
1.
2.

Gm7
Am7
B♭
Dm/F
Po - ki - noï, Po - ki - noï dji noch pre - do.
D.S. 𝄋 al Coda
Gm7
Am7
Dm
Dsus2 sus4
Dm
Os - ti - nyi du brach ti - vo.
𝄌 Coda
Dm
Ending:
Gm7
Am7
Po - ki - noï dji noch pre - do.
Po - ki - noï, Po - ki - noï
B♭
Dm/F
Gm7
Os - ti - nyi
dji noch pre - do.
Os - ti - nyi

Am7
Dm
Dsus2
sus4
Dm
du brach_ ti - vo.
du_ brach_ ti - vo.

Dm9
3
Po - ki - noï.

Repeat and fade